I0427767

Surface Moving Map Industry Survey

DOT-VNTSC-FAA-09-15

Air Traffic Organization Operations Planning

Human Factors Research and Engineering Group

Washington, DC 20591

Michelle Yeh

Danielle Eon

U.S. Department of Transportation

Research and Innovative Technology Administration

John A. Volpe National Transportation Systems Center

Cambridge, MA 02142

August 2009

Notice

This document is disseminated under the sponsorship of the Department of Transportation in the interest of information exchange. The United States Government assumes no liability for its contents or use thereof.

Notice

The United States Government does not endorse products or manufacturers. Trade or manufacturers' names appear herein solely because they are considered essential to the objective of this report.

REPORT DOCUMENTATION PAGE

Form Approved
OMB No. 0704-0188

Public reporting burden for this collection of information is estimated to average 1 hour per response, including the time for reviewing instructions, searching existing data sources, gathering and maintaining the data needed, and completing and reviewing the collection of information. Send comments regarding this burden estimate or any other aspect of this collection of information, including suggestions for reducing this burden, to Washington Headquarters Services, Directorate for Information Operations and Reports, 1215 Jefferson Davis Highway, Suite 1204, Arlington, VA 22202-4302, and to the Office of Management and Budget, Paperwork Reduction Project (0704-0188), Washington, DC 20503.

1. AGENCY USE ONLY (Leave blank)	2. REPORT DATE August 2009	3. REPORT TYPE AND DATES COVERED Final Report
4. TITLE AND SUBTITLE Surface Moving Map Industry Survey		5. FUNDING NUMBERS FA6Y/ED8T6 FA6Y/FD8T6 FA6YC1/ FD5RF FA6YC2/ FD276
6. AUTHOR(S) Michelle Yeh and Danielle Eon		
7. PERFORMING ORGANIZATION NAME(S) AND ADDRESS(ES) U.S. Department of Transportation John A. Volpe National Transportation Systems Center Research and Innovative Technology Administration Cambridge, MA 02142-1093		8. PERFORMING ORGANIZATION REPORT NUMBER DOT-VNTSC-FAA-09-15
9. SPONSORING/MONITORING AGENCY NAME(S) AND ADDRESS(ES) U.S. Department of Transportation Federal Aviation Administration Air Traffic Organization Operations Planning Human Factors Research and Engineering Group 800 Independence Avenue, SW Washington, D.C. 20591 Program Manager: Dr. Tom McCloy		10. SPONSORING/MONITORING AGENCY REPORT NUMBER
11. SUPPLEMENTARY NOTES		
12a. DISTRIBUTION/AVAILABILITY STATEMENT This document is available to the public through the National Technical Information Service, Springfield, VA 22161		12b. DISTRIBUTION CODE

13. ABSTRACT (Maximum 200 words)

This industry survey provides an overview of the currently available surface moving map products, as of March, 2009. Thirteen manufacturers and six research organizations participated and provided descriptions of the information elements they depict and the functions they are implementing. This report was conducted in support of the Federal Aviation Administration (FAA) but the information is intended to be of use to anyone interested in surface moving map display products.

This industry survey is divided into three sections. The first describes the method for the survey and summarizes the capabilities offered by manufacturers and research organizations. The second contains detailed information tables for the products currently available or in development by avionics manufacturers, and the third provides information tables for research organizations. References to both policy and research documents are listed at the end of this document.

14. SUBJECT TERM surface moving map, airport moving map display, electronic map display, avionics, industry survey, flight deck technology, moving map display, airport map		15. NUMBER OF PAGES 86
		16. PRICE CODE

17. SECURITY CLASSIFICATION OF REPORT Unclassified	18. SECURITY CLASSIFICATION OF THIS PAGE Unclassified	19. SECURITY CLASSIFICATION OF ABSTRACT Unclassified	20. LIMITATION OF ABSTRACT

This page left blank intentionally.

PREFACE

This report was prepared by the Behavioral Safety Research and Demonstration Division of the Human Factors Research and Systems Applications Center of Innovation at the John A. Volpe National Transportation Systems Center (Volpe Center). It was completed with funding from the Federal Aviation Administration's (FAA) Human Factors Research and Engineering Group (AJP-61) in support of the Aircraft Certification Service Avionics Branch (AIR-130) and the Technical Programs and Continued Airworthiness Branch (AIR-120). We would like to thank our FAA program manager, Dr. Tom McCloy, as well as our technical sponsor, Colleen Donovan, for providing suggestions and feedback. Many thanks also to Caroline Donohoe who helped coordinate the manufacturers' responses to this request, to Young-Jin Jo and Andrew Kendra who provided feedback on this report, and to the many manufacturers who generously provided information for the industry survey.

The views expressed herein are those of the authors and do not necessarily reflect the views of the Volpe National Transportation Systems Center, the Research and Innovative Technology Administration, or the United States Department of Transportation.

Feedback on this document can be sent to Michelle Yeh (Michelle.Yeh@dot.gov).

METRIC/ENGLISH CONVERSION FACTORS

ENGLISH TO METRIC

METRIC TO ENGLISH

LENGTH (APPROXIMATE)

1 inch (in) = 2.5 centimeters (cm)
1 foot (ft) = 30 centimeters (cm)
1 yard (yd) = 0.9 meter (m)
1 mile (mi) = 1.6 kilometers (km)

LENGTH (APPROXIMATE)

1 millimeter (mm) = 0.04 inch (in)
1 centimeter (cm) = 0.4 inch (in)
1 meter (m) = 3.3 feet (ft)
1 meter (m) = 1.1 yards (yd)
1 kilometer (km) = 0.6 mile (mi)

AREA (APPROXIMATE)

1 square inch (sq in, in^2) = 6.5 square centimeters (cm^2)
1 square foot (sq ft, ft^2) = 0.09 square meter (m^2)
1 square yard (sq yd, yd^2) = 0.8 square meter (m^2)
1 square mile (sq mi, mi^2) = 2.6 square kilometers (km^2)
1 acre = 0.4 hectare (he) = 4,000 square meters (m^2)

AREA (APPROXIMATE)

1 square centimeter (cm^2) = 0.16 square inch (sq in, in^2)
1 square meter (m^2) = 1.2 square yards (sq yd, yd^2)
1 square kilometer (km^2) = 0.4 square mile (sq mi, mi^2)
10,000 square meters (m^2) = 1 hectare (ha) = 2.5 acres

MASS - WEIGHT (APPROXIMATE)

1 ounce (oz) = 28 grams (gm)
1 pound (lb) = 0.45 kilogram (kg)
1 short ton = 2,000 pounds (lb) = 0.9 tonne (t)

MASS - WEIGHT (APPROXIMATE)

1 gram (gm) = 0.036 ounce (oz)
1 kilogram (kg) = 2.2 pounds (lb)
1 tonne (t) = 1,000 kilograms (kg) = 1.1 short tons

VOLUME (APPROXIMATE)

1 teaspoon (tsp) = 5 milliliters (ml)
1 tablespoon (tbsp) = 15 milliliters (ml)
1 fluid ounce (fl oz) = 30 milliliters (ml)
1 cup (c) = 0.24 liter (l)
1 pint (pt) = 0.47 liter (l)
1 quart (qt) = 0.96 liter (l)
1 gallon (gal) = 3.8 liters (l)
1 cubic foot (cu ft, ft^3) = 0.03 cubic meter (m^3)
1 cubic yard (cu yd, yd^3) = 0.76 cubic meter (m^3)

VOLUME (APPROXIMATE)

1 milliliter (ml) = 0.03 fluid ounce (fl oz)
1 liter (l) = 2.1 pints (pt)
1 liter (l) = 1.06 quarts (qt)
1 liter (l) = 0.26 gallon (gal)
1 cubic meter (m^3) = 36 cubic feet (cu ft, ft^3)
1 cubic meter (m^3) = 1.3 cubic yards (cu yd, yd^3)

TEMPERATURE (EXACT)

$[(x-32)(5/9)]$ °F = y °C

TEMPERATURE (EXACT)

$[(9/5) y + 32]$ °C = x °F

QUICK INCH - CENTIMETER LENGTH CONVERSION

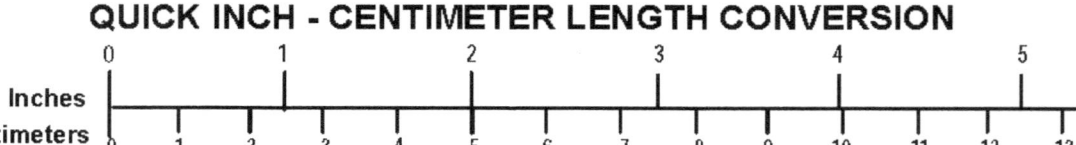

QUICK FAHRENHEIT - CELSIUS TEMPERATURE CONVERSION

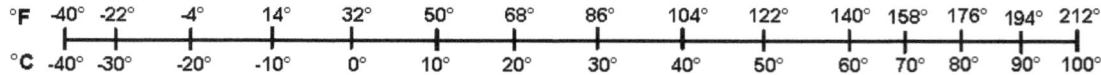

For more exact and or other conversion factors, see NIST Miscellaneous Publication 286, Units of Weights and Measures. Price $2.50 SD Catalog No. C13 10286 Updated 6/17/98

Table of Contents

This page left blank intentionally.

Executive Summary

This industry survey provides an overview of currently available surface moving map products, as of March, 2009. This report was conducted in support of the Federal Aviation Administration (FAA) but the information is intended to be of use to anyone interested in surface moving map displays. Thirteen manufacturers and six research organizations participated in this industry survey. Each provided a description of the airport information elements depicted and functions being implemented. For each product, the manufacturer's website is provided where more up-to-date information may be found.

This industry survey is divided into three main sections. The first describes the method for the survey and provides a summary of capabilities offered by manufacturers and research organizations. The second contains detailed information tables for products currently available or in development by avionics manufacturers, and the third provides information tables for research organizations. The material in these sections was gathered through collaboration with the participants and from information provided at demonstrations or in websites or brochures. A picture of each application is provided, where available. For manufacturer displays, information on FAA approvals received or in progress is also included. References to both policy and research documents are listed at the end of this document.

This page left blank intentionally.

Acronyms

AC	Advisory Circular
ADS-B	Automatic Dependent Surveillance-Broadcast
AIR	FAA Office of Aircraft Certification
AMDB	Aerodrome Moving Map Database
ATC	Air Traffic Control
CAA	Civil Aviation Authority
CAST	Commercial Aviation Safety Team
CDTI	Cockpit Display of Traffic Information
CFR	Code of Federal Regulations
CPDLC	Controller Pilot Data Link Communications
DP	Departure Procedures
EASA	European Aviation Safety Agency
EFB	Electronic Flight Bag
EFIS	Electronic Flight Instrument System
EPGWS	Enhanced Ground Proximity Warning System
FAA	Federal Aviation Administration
FMS	Flight Management System
FSB	Flight Standardization Board
GPS	Global Positioning System
HDU	Hard Disc Unit
JSIT	Joint Safety Implementation Team
LCD	Liquid Crystal Display
MFD	Multi-Function Display
NACO	National Aeronautical Charting Office
ND	Navigation Display
NOTAM	Notices to Airmen
PC	Personal Computer
PDA	Personal Digital Assistant
PFD	Primary Flight Display
PID	Pilot Information Display
SC	Steering Committee
SMM	Surface Moving Map
SST	Solid State Tablet
STAR	Standard Terminal Arrival Routes
STC	Supplemental Type Certificate
SVGA	Super Video Graphics Adapter/Array
TAC	Terminal Area Charts

TAWS	Terrain Awareness System
TCAS	Traffic Alert Collision Avoidance System
TFT	Thin-Film Transistor (screens)
TIS-B	Traffic Information Service – Broadcast
TSO	Technical Standard Order
US	United States
WAAS	Wide Area Augmentation System
WAC	World Aeronautical Charts
WG	Working Group

1   INTRODUCTION

Many manufacturers are developing moving map displays that show ownship position on the airport surface. The implementation of these displays varies widely in terms of what airport information elements they depict and what functions they can do. The Federal Aviation Administration (FAA) provides guidance for the design and approval of the surface moving map application in Technical Standard Order (TSO)-C165, *Electronic Map Display Equipment for Graphical Depiction of Aircraft Position*, which was issued on September 30, 2003 [7]. TSO-C165 defines minimum performance standards for electronic map displays, and it applies to equipment that is intended to provide ownship position on an electronic map display, whether it is on the airport surface, in-flight, or vertical situation display. Additional guidance to streamline the approval process for using a surface moving map application on an Electronic Flight Bag (EFB) is provided in Advisory Circular (AC) 20-159, *Obtaining Design and Production Approval of Airport Moving Map Display Applications Intended for Electronic Flight Bag Systems*, which was issued on April 30, 2007 [2]. Both TSO-C165 and AC 20-159 reference RTCA DO-257A, *Minimum Operational Performance Standards for the Depiction of Navigational Information on Electronic Maps*, which provides additional guidance for the design and evaluation of surface moving map displays [9]. General display guidance is contained in AC 25-11A, *Electronic Flight Deck Displays* [3].

This industry survey provides an overview of currently available surface moving map products, as of March, 2009. This survey updates two earlier efforts: one conducted in 2004 (see [17] for more information), and a second, which was primarily an informal update, in which manufacturers who participated in the 2004 survey were contacted in November, 2006, to identify product changes. Manufacturers and research organizations were identified for this industry survey based on previous participation, presentations at industry meetings (e.g., RTCA Steering Committee (SC)-186, working group (WG)-1), and a web search.

In total, 13 manufacturers and 6 research organizations participated in this industry survey. Although all efforts were made to provide as comprehensive a review as possible, it is important to note that there are other ongoing efforts that are not included in this document. Some manufacturers declined to participate or did not respond to the invitation. Manufacturers who only offer a third-party surface moving map are not explicitly listed here, since the surface moving map software is provided by another vendor. For example, Avidyne, Garmin, Honeywell, Rockwell Collins, and Universal Avionics have JeppView available for purchase on their product lines. However, some these companies do not offer their own surface moving map (in addition to JeppView), so they are not all included in this report.

This industry survey is divided into three sections. The first describes the method for the survey and summarizes the capabilities offered by manufacturers and research organizations. The second contains detailed information tables for products currently available or in development by avionics manufacturers, and the third provides information tables for research organizations. The material in these sections was gathered through collaboration with the participants and from information provided at demonstrations or in websites or brochures. A picture of each application is provided. For manufacturer displays, information on FAA approvals received or in progress is also included. References to both policy and research documents are included at the end of this document.

2   TECHNICAL APPROACH

2.1   Participants

The manufacturers and research organizations who contributed information on their surface moving map display efforts are listed in two tables. Table 1 lists participating manufacturers, the product(s) offered, and a website where more information can be found. Table 2 lists research organizations, the research display, and a website. Although the surface moving map applications used by research organizations may not be a product in itself, the results of these efforts are publicly available and manufacturers may incorporate some of the lessons learned. It is also worth noting that some of the activities conducted by these research organizations were done in close partnership with industry.

Table 1. Participating manufacturers.

Manufacturer	Product	Website
Airbus Toulouse, France	On Board Airport Navigation System (OANS)	www.airbus.com
AirGator Mount Kisko, NY	NavAir Approaches 3D	www.airgator.com
Astronautics Corporation of America Milwaukee, Wisconsin	Cockpit Display of Traffic Information (CDTI) Universal Cockpit Display of Traffic Information (UCDTI)	www.astronautics.com
Aviation Communication and Surveillance Systems (ACSS) Phoenix, AZ	SafeRoute	www.l-3com.com/acss/
FlightPrep Aurora, OR	ChartCase Professional, ChartCase Express	www.flightprep.com
Garmin Olathe, KS	SafeTaxi	www.garmin.com
Honeywell Phoenix, AZ	SmartRunway (Runway Awareness and Advisory System - RAAS) Note: RAAS supports aural alerts. A visual component, textual messages, will be supported beginning in 2009.	www.honeywell.com Runway Awareness and Advisory System (RAAS)
Jeppesen Denver, CO	Jeppesen Airport Moving Map software and database for EFB systems	www.jeppesen.com Airport Moving Map Overview
	JeppView (FliteDeck and MFD)	www.jeppesen.com
Lufthansa Systems Frankfurt, Germany	Lido Airport Moving Map	www.lhsystems.com
MAPTECH Aeronautical Data Exeter, NH	GENESYS SMM	www.dacint.com
Rockwell Collins, Inc. Cedar Rapids, IA	A moving map implementation displaying airport surface, ownship, traffic, and runway related indications and traffic conflict alerts. Additionally, taxi route, taxi clearance limit, route deviation alert and clearance deviation alert are available (if taxi route and clearance limit information is made available).	www.rockwellcollins.com

Table 1. Participating manufacturers. (continued)

Manufacturer	Product	Website
TerraVision Petah Tikva, Israel	FollowTheGreen	www.terravision.co.il
Thales Toulouse, France	Airport Navigation Product Line	www.thalesgroup.com OANS (Onboard Airport Navigation System)

Table 2. Participating research organizations.

Research Organization	Research Display	Website
BAE Systems Technische Universität Darmstadt (AMM Developer) University of Malta Deep Blue	Airborne Integrated Systems for Safety Improvement, Flight Hazard Protection and All Weather Operations (FLYSAFE)	www.eu-flysafe.org
Delft University of Technology Delft, The Netherlands	Safe Airport Navigation	• www.synthetic-vision.tudelft.nl/SVat DelftUofT/SVatDelftUofT.htm • www.stw.nl/Projecten/D/det/det5844. htm
MITRE McLean, VA	MITRE CAASD Cockpit Display of Traffic Information (CDTI) prototype	www.mitre.org
NASA-Ames Research Center Moffet Field, CA	Taxiway Navigation and Situation Awareness (T-NASA) System	• NASA-Ames Human Factors: humansystems.arc.nasa.gov/ • T-NASA: hsi.arc.nasa.gov/groups/HCSL/ research/tnasa.html • Research reports: hsi.arc.nasa.gov/groups/HCSL/ publications.html
NASA-Langley Hampton, VA	Runway Incursion Prevention System (RIPS)	• www.nasa.gov/centers/langley/ho me/index.html • www.nasa.gov/centers/langley/ news/factsheets/RIPS.html Work conducted under a cooperative agreement with ERA (see www.erabeyondradar.com)
Technische Universität Darmstadt Darmstadt, Germany	Airport Moving Map	www.fsr.tu-darmstadt.de/research/ groups/en_cavok.html

2.2 Method

To gather information for this industry survey, the Volpe Center worked with a representative from each of the participating manufacturers and research organizations. The information collected was intended to highlight aspects of the interface (e.g., the information depicted and the interactivity provided) rather than the technical aspects of implementation. Each participant was asked for the following information regarding their product lines:

- Product name
- Website(s) where more information can be found. The text is hyperlinked to the manufacturer's site.
- Any FAA approvals received or in progress
- A brief overview of the product

- Characteristics of the hardware system(s) on which the application can be displayed (i.e., EFB, Flight Management System (FMS), or Multi-Function Display (MFD))
- Data format: Geo-referenced electronic chart or database driven
- Update rate
- Airport information elements depicted and the method of depiction
- Functions supported and methods of interaction. Functions of interest included ownship depiction, traffic depiction, any visual or auditory indications or alerts, and route guidance. Methods for interaction addressed decluttering, panning, and zooming.

A table containing this information for each participant was initially drafted by the Volpe Center based on previous information obtained from industry contacts, demonstrations, websites, and brochures. This draft table was sent to a representative at each participating company or research organization to review and edit, as needed. This document reflects the results of this collaborative effort.

2.3 Industry Overview

The information collected is summarized in four tables below. Table 3 describes the approval sought or compliance demonstrated by each surface moving map manufacturer. Table 4 provides information about the data format of the surface moving map and the industry standards with which the data format complies. Table 5 describes the information elements shown on the surface moving map applications included in this industry survey and their method of depiction. In some cases, the method of depiction is customizable (e.g., by varying the color or the symbol used to represent a display element), so only one implementation is described. Table 6 lists functions available or planned.

Detailed tables for each manufacturer are provided in Section 3 and for each research organization in Section 4. Images of the surface moving map implementations are also included in these sections.

Table 3. Summary of approval/compliance for manufacturers.

This table summarizes the approval sought or compliance demonstrated for each surface moving map manufacturer. Three key areas are highlighted.

- *Avionics box type*, i.e., whether the surface moving map is hosted on an installed display or on an EFB
- *Authority* providing the approval: FAA, EASA, Other
- Type of *approval/compliance*, e.g., TSOs, ACs, STC. Seven documents related to the surface moving map application or the hardware on which it may be hosted are specifically listed in the table.
  - TSO C-113, *Airborne Multipurpose Electronic Displays*, issued on October 27, 1986
  - TSO-C165, *Electronic Map Display Equipment for Graphical Depiction of Aircraft Position*, issued on September 30, 2003
  - TSO C-166A, *Extended Squitter Automatic Dependent Surveillance - Broadcast (ADS-B) and Traffic Information Service - Broadcast (TIS-B) Equipment Operating on the Radio Frequency of 1090 Megahertz (MHz)*, issued on December 21, 2006
  - AC 20-159, *Obtaining Design and Production Approval of Airport Moving Map Display Applications Intended for Electronic Flight Bag Systems*, issued on April 30, 2007
  - AC 120-76A, *Guidelines for the Certification, Airworthiness, and Operational Approval of Electronic Flight Bag Computing Devices*, issued on March 17, 2003
  - Order 8900.1, *Flight Standards Information Management System*, Electronic Flight Bag Operational Authorization Process (Volume 4, Chapter 15)
  - RTCA DO-178B, *Software Considerations in Airborne Systems and Equipment Certification*

The status of the approval or compliance is indicated using two symbols: a filled circle (●) indicates that the approval or compliance has been received, whereas an open circle (○) indicates that the manufacturer is in the process of seeking approval or demonstrating compliance. Empty cells indicate no approval or compliance.

Note that the table lists manufacturers only; information for research organizations was not included since they generally do not seek approval/compliance for their surface moving map displays.

Table 3. Summary of approval/compliance for manufacturers. (continued)

Manufacturer	Avionics Box Type				Authority			Approval/Compliance											
	Installed/MFD	EFB			FAA	EASA	Other	TSO				AC 20-159	AC 120-76A	TC	STC	Aircraft	Order 8900.1	RTCA DO-178B	Other
		Class 1	Class 2	Class 3				C113	C165	C166A	Other								
Airbus On Board Airport Navigation System (OANS)	✓				✓	✓								● (A380) ○	○	A380; A320, A330/340, A350 XWB		C	
AirGator NavAir Approaches 3D			✓		✓				○			○	○			○ (AW139 B737)	○		
Astronautics Corporation of America Cockpit Display of Traffic Information (CDTI)				✓	✓								●		●	UPS B757/767		B	
Universal Cockpit Display of Traffic Information (UCDTI)			✓	✓	✓				○			●	●					B	
Aviation Communication and Surveillance Systems (ACSS), SafeRoute			✓	✓	✓				●	●[1]		○	●		●	B757, B767		D / C	
FlightPrep ChartCase Professional, ChartCase Express		✓	✓		✓								●						AC 91-78, N8900.17
Garmin SafeTaxi	✓				✓	✓		●										D	
Honeywell SmartRunway	✓				✓					C151									

[1] With deviation.

Table 3. Summary of approval/compliance for manufacturers. (continued)

Manufacturer	Avionics Box Type				Authority			Approval/Compliance											
	Installed/ MFD	EFB			FAA	EASA	Other	TSO				AC 20-159	AC 120-76A	TC	STC	Aircraft	Order 8900.1	RTCA DO-178B	Other
		Class 1	Class 2	Class 3				C113	C165	C166A	Other								
Jeppesen																			
Jeppesen Airport Moving Map software and database for EFB systems			✓	✓	✓				●			●	●				●	D	
JeppView (FliteDeck and MFD)	Responsibility of the end user																		
Lufthansa Systems Lido Airport Moving Map			✓	✓	✓	✓			o			o	o				o	D	
MAPTECH Aeronautical Data GENESYS SMM			✓	✓	✓			●	o	o		o	●		●	CRJ, ERJ, DHC-8, B767L382, DC-8, B737, B777, Hawker/Beechcraft	●	C	
Rockwell Collins, Inc. Moving map implementation			✓				Swedish CAA								●	B737 NG		D²	
TerraVision FollowTheGreen ✈		✓	✓		✓		Israel CAA		o									D	
Thales Airport Navigation Product Line	✓				✓	✓								●		A380		C	

² Designed to meet the requirements specified but not approved.

Table 4. Data format and compliance to database standards.

The surface map may be a *geo-referenced electronic raster chart*, a *vector chart*, or a *database-driven display*. The first two data formats provide an airport depiction similar to what is shown on a pre-composed paper chart with some features verified for latitude/longitude accuracy. *Raster* charts are usually produced by scanning paper charts (or portions of paper charts) into an image format. The raster chart will be non-interactive if the full chart is scanned as one image, but groups of display elements may be stored as objects that can be manipulated. On a *vector* chart, every symbol is stored as an individual object so that lines and symbols can be redrawn as the pilot zooms in and out; this can help produce a clearer image. The third data format, a *database-driven display*, is constructed from a database that contains positional data describing the location of individual airport attributes. The surface moving map display is drawn in real time; they can vary in the detail with which the airport surface is depicted from one manufacturer to another and can support a great deal of interactivity.

Several standards provide assurance on the quality and accuracy of the data used to construct the surface moving map display; compliance with three standards are specifically listed in the table.

- ARINC Specification 816, *Embedded interchange Format for Airport Mapping Database*
- RTCA DO-200A, *Standards for Processing Aeronautical Data*
- RTCA DO-272/ED-99, *User Requirements for Aerodrome Mapping Information*

A filled circle (●) indicates the data format and compliance for current products; an open circle (○) indicates that the product is in development or that the manufacturer is in the process of demonstrating compliance.

Table 4. Data format and compliance to database standards. (continued)

	Data Format			Compliance to Database Standards			Other
	Raster chart	Vector chart	Database	ARINC 816	RTCA DO-200A	RTCA DO-272/ED-99	
Airbus On Board Airport Navigation System (OANS)			●	●	●		
AirGator NavAir Approaches 3D	●	○	○	●			
Astronautics Corporation of America							ARINC 424
Cockpit Display of Traffic Information (CDTI)			●	●			
Universal Cockpit Display of Traffic Information (UCDTI)			●	●			
Aviation Communication and Surveillance Systems (ACSS), SafeRoute			●	●	●	●	
FlightPrep ChartCase Professional, ChartCase Express	●	●					
Garmin SafeTaxi			●		●		
Honeywell SmartRunway			●				
Jeppesen							
Jeppesen Airport Moving Map software and database for EFB systems			●		●	●	
JeppView (FliteDeck and MFD)		●					
Lufthansa Systems Lido Airport Moving Map			●	●	●	●	
MAPTECH Aeronautical Data GENESYS SMM	●	●	●		●	●	
Rockwell Collins, Inc. Moving map implementation			●				
TerraVision FollowTheGreen			●	●	●	●	
Thales Airport Navigation Product Line			●			●	RTCA DO-160D RTCA DO-254 Level C

Table 5. Display elements. A dash (--) indicates that the information element is not depicted.

	Participants	Runways	Runway Centerlines	Runway Labels	Taxiways	Taxiway Centerlines	Taxiway Labels
Manufacturer Displays	**Airbus**	White	White	White	Grey	Yellow	Yellow text in black text boxes
	AirGator	Black	--	Black	Grey	--	Black
	Astronautics*	Light grey with white border	White dashed lines	Blue text in black text boxes with blue border	Grey	--	Blue
	ACSS (Aviation Communication and Surveillance Systems)	Dark grey, white border	White dashed lines	Blue text in black text boxes	Dark grey	--	Blue
	FlightPrep	Black	--	Black	Grey	--	Black
	Garmin	White	Grey dotted lines	White text in black text boxes	Grey	--	White text in black text boxes
	Honeywell	N/A. SmartRunway (RAAS) does not support ownship display.					
	Jeppesen Airport Moving Map	Light grey	White	Blue text in blue oval with black background	Dark grey	--	White
	JeppView	Black	--	Black	Grey	--	Black
	Lufthansa Systems	Light grey	Black dashed line	Black	Grey	Yellow line	White
	MAPTECH Aeronautical Data	Light grey	White	White	Dark grey	Yellow	White
	Rockwell-Collins	Grey	White	Black text in white text boxes	Grey	White	White characters in blue text boxes
	TerraVision	Light grey	White	White text in dark grey text boxes	Dark grey	Yellow	Yellow text in black box
	Thales*	White	Yes	White	Grey	Yes	Yellow text in black box
Research Displays	**BAE Systems, Technische Universität Darmstadt, University of Malta, Deep Blue**	Light grey	White	White text in black text box	Dark grey	Yellow	Yellow text in black text box
	Delft University of Technology	Grey	--	Black text in white text boxes	Grey	Grey	White text in blue text boxes
	MITRE	Dark grey	White	White	Light grey	--	White text in black text box
	NASA-Ames Research Center	Black	--	White	Black	--	White
	NASA-Langley*	Grey	White	Yellow	Brown	--	Yellow
	Technische Universität Darmstadt	Light grey	White	White text in a black text box	Dark grey	Yellow	Yellow text in black text box

* The method of depiction may vary. Only one implementation is described here.

Table 5. Display elements. (continued)

	Participants	Hold Lines	Non-Movement Areas	Ramp Areas	Grassy Areas	Buildings	Building Labels
Manufacturer Display	Airbus	Red	Black	Black	Black	Blue	Blue
	AirGator	--	White	Grey	White	Black	Black
	Astronautics*	--	Black	Dark grey	Black	Brown cross-hatched pattern	--
	ACSS	Yellow	Black	Dark grey	Black	Brown border with cross-hatched fill	--
	FlightPrep	--	White	Grey	White	Black	Black
	Garmin	--	Green	Grey	Green	Black	Black text
	Honeywell	N/A. SmartRunway (RAAS) does not support ownship display.					
	Jeppesen Airport Moving Map	Amber	Dirt and grass areas in black; blast pads and overrun areas in light grey	Dark grey	Black	Blue	White text
	JeppView	--	White	Grey	White	Black	Black text
	Lufthansa Systems	Yellow line	Black	Grey	Black	Brown	White
	MAPTECH Aeronautical Data	Yellow	Black	Light grey	Green	Brown	White
	Rockwell-Collins	Yellow	Grey	Grey	Green	Black	--
	TerraVision	Tomato	Black	Dark grey	Black	Blue	White
	Thales*	Yes	Black	Grey	Black	Blue	Blue in black box
Research Displays	BAE Systems, Technische Universität Darmstadt, University of Malta, Deep Blue	Red	Black	Dark grey	Black	Blue	--
	Delft University of Technology	Yellow	Grey	Grey	Green	Black	--
	MITRE	--	Black	Black	Black	Blue	--
	NASA-Ames Research Center	Red bar surrounded by yellow border	Black	Black	Green	Blue	--
	NASA-Langley*	--	Black	Black	Green	Brown	--
	Technische Universität Darmstadt	Yellow	Black	Dark grey	Black	Blue	--

* The method of depiction may vary. Only one implementation is described here.

Table 6. Functionality. A dash (--) indicates that the function is not available.

	Participants	Ownship Depiction	Traffic Display	Route Guidance	Decluttering	Panning	Zooming/ Autozoom
Manufacturer Displays	Airbus	Magenta aircraft icon	In development	In development	x	x	x
	AirGator	Red triangle	x	In development	x	x	x
	Astronautics	Magenta triangle outlined with white border	x	x	x	x	x
	ACSS	Magenta triangle	x	--	x	--	x
	FlightPrep	User customizable	--	--	x	x	x
	Garmin	Airplane icon	x	--	x	x	x
	Honeywell	N/A	x	--	x	--	--
	Jeppesen Airport Moving Map	Amber chevron (class 2) Isosceles triangle (class 3)	--	--	x	x	x
	JeppView	FliteDeck: Green chevron MFD: Varies depending on manufacturer	--	--	--	x	x
	Lufthansa Systems	Orange chevron	--	x	x	x	x
	MAPTECH Aeronautical Data	User customizable	--	x	--	x	x
	Rockwell-Collins	White triangle at high map ranges; white aircraft icon when map range is 400 m or less	x	x	x	x	x
	TerraVision	Green triangle. Green circle at low speeds or when heading is unreliable.	In development	In development	x	x	x
	Thales	Aircraft symbol (typically purple or yellow)	In development	x	x	x	x

12

Table 6. Functionality. (continued)

	Participants	Ownship Depiction	Traffic Display	Route Guidance	Decluttering	Panning	Zooming/ Autozoom
Research Displays	BAE Systems, Technische Universität Darmstadt, University of Malta, Deep Blue	Yellow aircraft icon	x	x	x	--	x
	Delft University of Technology	White triangle at high map ranges; white aircraft icon when closely zoomed in	x	x	x	x	x
	MITRE	White unfilled triangle	x	--	--	--	x
	NASA-Ames Research Center	White triangular symbol	x	x	x	--	x
	NASA-Langley	White triangle (solid when on ground; unfilled when airborne)	x	x	x	--	x
	Technische Universität Darmstadt	Yellow aircraft icon	x	x	x	--	x

3   MANUFACTURER DISPLAYS

Airbus	Location: Toulouse, France
Product(s)	OANS (On Board Airport Navigation System)
Website(s)	www.airbus.com
Approvals / Compliance	*Avionics Box Type :* ☒ Installed/MFD ☐ EFB (Class ☐ 1 ☐ 2 ☐ 3) *Authority:* ☒ FAA ☒ EASA ☐ Other *Type of Approval/Compliance* TSO: ☐ C113 ☐ C165 ☐ C166A ☐ Other AC: ☐ AC 20-159 ☐ AC120-76A ☒ TC ☐ STC *Aircraft:* __A380__ Note: Approvals for A320, A330/340 and A350XWB families in progress. ☐ Order 8900.1 ☒ RTCA DO-178B (Level C)

Product Overview

The OANS (On Board Airport Navigation System) provides the flight crew with information regarding the aircraft's localisation on the airport surface. This is realized by displaying an electronic moving airport map, positioned and oriented relative to an aircraft symbol that represents ownship's position. Three different display modes are provided (ARC, ROSE, PLAN), similar to what is available on the navigation display (ND). In addition, the electronic moving airport map function displays a set of information such as the name of the displayed airport, taxiways, runways, gates, buildings, and current ground speed. Notched zooming with different level of details (decluttering function). Manual map displacement (i.e., panning), map annotations and search functions (e.g., "taxiway P20") are also provided. The OANS is certified on A380 and under development for A320, A330/340 and A350XWB families. Integrated in avionics, it supports other aircraft functions (e.g., Brake to Vacate, Runway Overrun Protection).

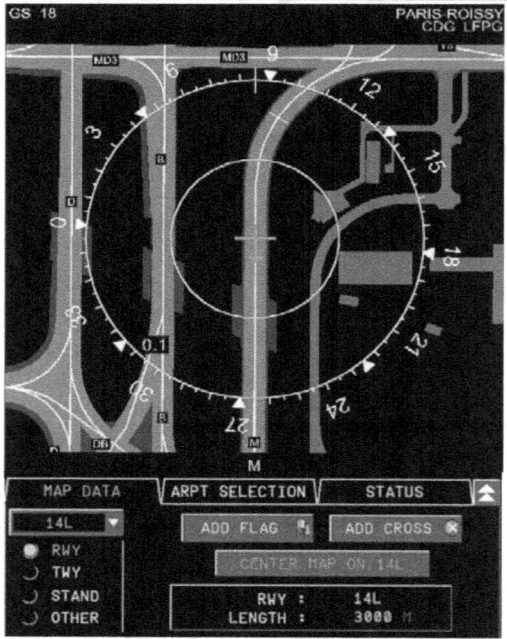

Copyright AIRBUS S.A.S. Not to be reproduced without permission.

Hardware Platform	The OANS is presented on the Navigation Display
Display Size	- A380 : Display diagonal is 10" / Display resolution is 1024 x 768 - A320/A330/A340 : Display diagonal is 8.5" / Display resolution is 756 x 756 - A350XWB : Display diagonal is 10" / Display resolution is 990 x 720

Airbus		**Location:** Toulouse, France
Data Format	☐ Raster ☐ Vector ☒ Database *Format* ☒ ARINC Specification 816 *Standards* ☒ RTCA DO-200A ☐ RTCA DO-272 *Other:* Varies depending on the avionics and/or display platform	
Update Rate	The computed aircraft position is updated and refreshed on the displays at a rate of 15 Hz	

Airport Information Elements Depicted

Runways	White
Runway centerlines	White
Runway labels	White text
Taxiways	Grey
Taxiway centerlines	Yellow
Taxiway labels	Yellow text in black text boxes
Hold lines	Red
Non-movement areas	Black
Ramp areas	Black
Grassy areas	Black
Buildings	Blue
Building labels	Blue
Other	

Functions Supported

Ownship Depiction	Ownship is depicted as a magenta aircraft icon ROSE mode 2 NM *Copyright AIRBUS S.A.S. Not to be reproduced without permission.*

Airbus	Location: Toulouse, France
Indicators	Runway proximity is approved. Others are in prototype phase (runway incursion, take off on taxiway, overspeed on taxiway, taxiway characteristics inadequate for aircraft...)
Conditions	Fine tuning underway
Visual Indicators	Runway proximity indicator is a visual only indicator on the navigation display (ND). Definition underway for the indications in prototype phase. Visual indicators will be implemented in accordance with flight deck alarm & colors philosophy
Auditory Indicators	Definition underway for indications in prototype phase. Auditory indicators will be integrated with cockpit audio warnings
Decluttering	Yes: Increasing the range will declutter the display
Panning	Yes: In all modes and ranges, the crew can displace the map in all directions by using simultaneously the validation pushbutton and the trackball (analogy with "click and drag" concept). In PLAN mode, the map stays at its position when the pushbutton is released. In ARC and ROSE NAV modes, the map automatically returns to the ARC and ROSE NAV disposition with respect to A/C, with smooth transition, as soon as the pushbutton is released.
Traffic Display	In prototype phase
Route Guidance	In prototype phase
Zooming/Autozoom	Zooming is provided via range selection. Available ranges are : 5Nm, 2Nm, 1NM, 0.5Nm and 0.2Nm Autozoom : prototype / concept evaluation phase

AirGator		Location:	Mount Kisco, NY
Product(s)	NAVAir Approaches3D		
Website(s)	www.airgator.com		
Approvals / Compliance	*Avionics Box Type* : ☐ Installed/MFD ☒ EFB (Class ☐ 1 ☒ 2 ☐ 3) *Authority*: ☒ FAA ☐ EASA ☐ Other *Type of Approval/Compliance* TSO: ☐ C113 ☐ C165 ☐ C166A ☐ Other AC: ☒ AC 20-159 ☒ AC120-76A ☐ TC ☒ STC *Aircraft*: AW139 B737 ☒ Order 8900.1 (In progress) ☐ RTCA DO-178B (Level ___) *Other Notes*: Seeking approval per FAA TSO C-165		

Product Overview

NAVAir Approaches3D provides a viewer for Instrument Approach Procedures and Airport Diagrams. All charts are geo-referenced, so that WAAS-driven aircraft GPS position and altitude can be shown. NavAir Approaches may be viewed on a panel-mounted displays, Electronic Flight Bags, desktop, laptop, tablet PC, or personal digital assistant (PDA).

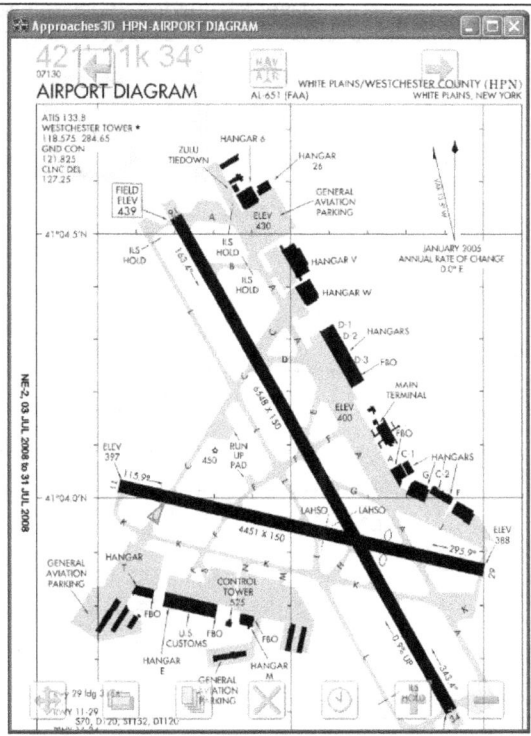

Photo courtesy of AirGator.

Hardware Platform	Class 1, 2 EFBs in both portable and installed configurations, panel mounted displays. Class 3 EFB installations are possible with appropriate equipment.

AirGator	Location: Mount Kisco, NY

Display Size	Varies by system. A few examples are listed below. NAVPad 8 (HDU and SST): 8.4" 800 x 600, 1.7 lb. NAVPad 10 (HDU and SST): 10.4" 1024 x 768 2.1 lb NAVPad 7 (HDU and SST): 7" 800 x 480 1.4 lb NAVPad 5 (SST): 4.8" 800 x 480 0.8 lb NAVPad ACD (SST), 6.4" 640x480 Panel Mounted
Data Format	☒ Raster ☒ Vector ☒ Database Vector-based and database-driven surface moving map applications are in development. *Format* ☒ ARINC Specification 816 *Standards* ☐ RTCA DO-200A ☐ RTCA DO-272
Update Rate	1 – 10 Hz subject to position sensor rates

Airport Information Elements Depicted

The information listed is based on the current implementation of the surface moving map application using geo-referenced NACO charts. Future versions using vector-based charts or database-driven formats are in development; these implementations will allow the user to define the colors and graphics for all airport information elements.

Runways	Black Note: The color of runways and runway outlines can be user-customized in the current implementation.
Runway centerlines	--
Runway labels	Black
Taxiways	Grey
Taxiway centerlines	--
Taxiway labels	Black
Hold lines	--
Non-movement areas	White
Ramp areas	Grey
Grassy areas	White
Buildings	Black
Building labels	Black
Other	

Functions Supported

Specify whether the following functions are supported and if so, how the information is depicted.

Ownship Depiction	Yes, the method of depiction (e.g., icon, color) is user-definable. It is shown as a red triangle in the figure above. Ownship position data is provided from WAAS or other onboard position sensors.

AirGator		Location:	Mount Kisco, NY
Indicators	Ability to graphically designate clearance including taxi route, holds, and destination runways. Holds are depicted with yellow lines across taxi/runway crossings per image below. Potential runway incursion is depicted by drawing red cross-hatches along the runways. *Photo courtesy of AirGator.*		
Conditions	Aircraft position, runway location and pilot or automatic-clearance entry		
Visual Indicators	Runway crossings for the destination runway may be designated with a solid yellow line at the runway-taxiway threshold. The depicted distance from the line to the runway does not reflect the actual distance from the hold line to the runway; rather, it is a user-defined threshold whose default value is based on the FAA specified distance for painting hold lines on taxiways with respect to runways. The method for distinguishing the assigned runway from other runways may be customized by the user. Currently, the assigned runway is highlighted with a green line pattern, as shown in the image below. If the airport has more than one runway, the runway(s) that are not relevant to the current route may be designated with a red line pattern overlay composed of dashes and dots. *Photo courtesy of AirGator.*		

AirGator	Location: Mount Kisco, NY
Auditory Indicators	User defined or system standard alerts may be activated for threshold crossings and arrival at designated destination runway. The form of the auditory indication is user-customizable and can range from a tone to a pre-recorded voice message.
Decluttering	Decluttering limited to alerts (on vs. off) and traffic (on vs. off)
Panning	Yes. Touchscreen or EFB/MFD bezel controls used to pan and jump to specific portions on the diagram
Traffic Display	Traffic is displayed from a variety of sources includes TCAS, ADS-B, Mode S and portable traffic alert devices with compatible output
Route Guidance	This function is currently in development. Pilot may designate taxi route by tapping on/selecting taxiway segments, intersections, and the destination runway. Automated taxi clearance depiction will be activated when automated clearance information is available. If the aircraft has been cleared to cross the runway, a yellow bar appears at the runway-taxiway threshold. If the aircraft has *not* yet been cleared, a line pattern of red x's is drawn at the runway-taxiway threshold.
Zooming/Autozoom	Zooming from 25% - 800% is supported in user defined increments. Autozoom is implemented for threshold crossings and designated problem areas.

Astronautics Corporation of America	**Location:**	Milwaukee, Wisconsin

Product(s)	Universal Cockpit Display of Traffic Information (UCDTI) Cockpit Display of Traffic Information (CDTI)		
Website(s)	www.astronautics.com		
CDTI **Approvals / Compliance**	*Avionics Box Type* : ☐ Installed/MFD ☒ EFB (Class ☐ 1 ☐ 2 ☒ 3) *Authority*: ☒ FAA ☐ EASA ☐ Other *Type of Approval/Compliance* TSO: ☐ C113 ☐ C165 ☐ C166A ☐ Other AC: ☐ AC 20-159 ☒ AC120-76A ☐ TC ☒ STC *Aircraft*: _UPS Boeing 757/767_ ☐ Order 8900.1 ☒ RTCA DO-178B (Level _B_)		
UCDTI **Approvals / Compliance**	*Avionics Box Type* : ☐ Installed/MFD ☒ EFB (Class ☐ 1 ☒ 2 ☒ 3) *Authority*: ☒ FAA ☐ EASA ☐ Other *Type of Approval/Compliance* TSO: ☐ C113 ☒ C165 (in process) ☐ C166A ☐ Other AC: ☒ AC 20-159 ☒ AC120-76A ☐ TC ☐ STC *Aircraft*: _____ ☐ Order 8900.1 ☒ RTCA DO-178B (Level _B_)		

Product Overview

CDTI and UCDTI are software applications that present ownship position on an airport surface map and the position of surrounding traffic. They were developed under an alliance between Astronautics Corporation of America and ACSS.

CDTI was designed specifically for the Boeing/Astronautics Class-3 EFB to support the ACSS SafeRoute applications of Surface Area Movement Management (SAMM), Runway Awareness, CDTI Assisted Visual Separation (CAVS) and Merging and Spacing (M&S). UCDTI is designed to provide similar functions as the CDTI application but it can be hosted on a variety of platforms and operating systems including any Class-3 and Class-2 Electronic Flight Bags (EFBs) running Windows or Linux operating systems or other compatible cockpit displays. UCDTI functions and interface are configurable to support different customer needs. For example, it can be operated independently, but it can also show airport traffic information when connected to an ADS-B surveillance processor, and it can be expanded to support the ACSS SafeRoute applications noted above when connected to an ACSS Surveillance processor.

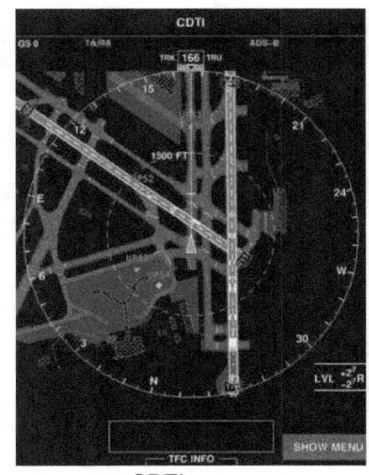
CDTI

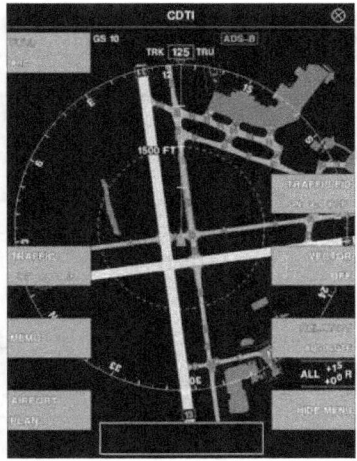
UCDTI

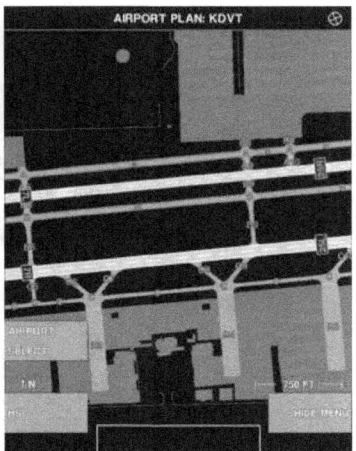
Airport Plan View (north-up)

Photos provided courtesy of Astronautics Corporation of America.

Astronautics Corporation of America		Location:	Milwaukee, Wisconsin

Hardware Platform	The CDTI application is designed to run on the Boeing/Astronautics Class 3 EFB. The UCDTI application can be hosted on a wide variety of platforms including any Class of EFB or other display systems running Windows or Linux operating systems. The UCDTI can be configured to use existing EFB bezel buttons including alpha-numeric keyboards, and is operable through touch screen or any other standard cursor control device.
Display Size	CDTI application is shown on a 6" x 8" portrait display with a resolution of 768 x 1024 pixels. UCDTI is configurable to support different display sizes (including rectangular and square displays, and portrait or landscape orientations). A resolution of at least 768 x 1024 pixels is recommended.
Data Format	☐ Raster ☐ Vector ☒ Database *Format* ☒ ARINC Specification 816 *Standards* ☐ RTCA DO-200A ☐ RTCA DO-272 *Other:* CDTI application also uses an ARINC-424 database for depiction of navigation fixes in conjunction with the Merging and Spacing function.
Update Rate	30 Hz; however the actual update rate is dependent on the hardware platform and other applications that may be sharing the same resources. A minimum of 15 Hz is allowed by the application before a safety monitor function reports loss of service.

Airport Information Elements Depicted

The information below reflects what is shown in the CDTI application. The information elements depicted and method of depiction for the UCDTI application will vary depending on the hardware graphics capabilities.

Runways	Light grey with white borders outlining the runway edges
Runway centerlines	White dashed lines
Runway labels	Blue text in a black text box. The text box is surrounded by a blue border
Taxiways	Grey
Taxiway centerlines	--
Taxiway labels	Blue
Hold lines	Yellow
Non-movement areas	Black
Ramp areas	Dark grey
Grassy areas	Black
Buildings	Brown cross-hatched pattern
Building labels	--
Other	The UCDTI application may be configured to present any element in the ARINC-816 database including closed taxiways and runways, helipads, water, etc.

Functions Supported

Own ship Depiction	Magenta triangle, outlined with a white border. Own ship position is presented in a track-up orientation. The UCDTI application also provides a north-up orientation.

Astronautics Corporation of America	Location:	Milwaukee, Wisconsin

Indicators	<ul><li>SAMM and Runway Awareness (the implementation of this function varies depending on the level of approval of the system on which it is hosted)</li><li>CDTI Assisted Visual Separation (CAVS) – Distance and differential ground speed to a coupled target during any phase of flight (CDTI only)</li><li>Merging and Spacing (M&S) – provide the flight crew with an M&S Command Speed target to achieve and maintain spacing at a selected time interval behind a designated traffic-to-follow (TTF) during the en route, descent, and arrival phases of flight. (CDTI only)</li></ul>
Conditions	Runway Indications – The tolerances for determining whether the own ship is aligned with a non-selected runway are configurable. (Growth provision, subject to FAA approval) CAVS – User may specify a range alerting distance. When the coupled target is within the selected range alerting distance, a RANGE ALERT message is displayed. M&S – User enters traffic to follow, desired spacing interval, merge waypoint, final approach speed, and range alerting distance.
Visual Indicators	Runway Indications – With runway indication, the UCDTI application highlights the selected runway, and will highlight a non-selected runway when the aircraft is oriented to a runway that is not selected. In addition to the highlighting, a "CHECK RUNWAY" message will be displayed. (Growth provision, subject to FAA approval) CAVS – RANGE ALERT message presented when coupled target is within the selected range alerting distance. M&S – Command speed is annunciated along with graphical fast/slow indicator. Correct spacing position is also indicated graphically on the traffic portion of the display. *Photo provided courtesy of Astronautics Corporation of America.*
Aural Indicators	None

Astronautics Corporation of America	Location: Milwaukee, Wisconsin
Decluttering	Ground Traffic, Airborne Traffic, or all Traffic can independently be removed from the display. Filtering of traffic based on altitude is also supported. Traffic Flight IDs and position vectors can also be independently selected for display. The airport map detail is also modified based on zoom setting, with more detail visible at higher resolution zoom settings.
Panning	Panning is available in the north-up plan-style view. Panning is accomplished using arrow controls on the EFB bezel.
Traffic Display	Surrounding traffic is depicted using TCAS, ADS-B airborne and ground, and TIS-B airborne targets when connected to an ARINC-735B surveillance processor. Traffic may be depicted with flight ID, relative or absolute altitude, altitude trend, and position vector.
Route Guidance	UCDTI is expandable to also include route indication.
Zooming/Autozoom	Zoom functionality is supported; the settings are configurable. The CDTI application provides 11 settings: 750 FT, 1500 FT, 3000 FT, 1 NM, 2.5 NM, 5 NM, 12.5 NM, 25 NM, 50 NM, 100 NM, and 150 NM.

ACSS	Location: Phoenix, AZ

Product(s)	SafeRoute™ / CDTI

Website(s)	• www.acss.com • www.acssonboard.com/products/saferoute/

Approvals / Compliance	*Avionics Box Type* : ☐ Installed/MFD ☒ EFB (Class ☐ 1 ☒ 2 ☒ 3) *Authority*: ☒ FAA ☐ EASA (soon) ☐ Other *Type of Approval/Compliance* TSO: ☐ C113 ☒ C165 ☒ C166A <u>with deviation</u> ☐ Other AC: ☒ AC 20-159 ☒ AC120-76A ☐ TC ☒ STC *Aircraft*: <u>B757, B767</u> ☐ Order 8900.1 ☒ RTCA DO-178B (Level C for Class III EFB, Level D for Class II EFB) • FAA Operational Approval of the use of SAMM displayed information by flight crew during surface operations • Pending FAA approval on a Class 2 EFB for the display of own ship and traffic on an airport surface moving map per AC20-159

Product Overview

SafeRoute™ is a portfolio of airborne and ground surveillance applications. SafeRoute surface applications include Surface Area Movement Management (SAMM) and Runway Awareness. The SAMM function is designed to support operations on the airport surface or near a runway surface up to 1,500 feet above ground level (AGL). SAMM shows ownship's position and surrounding traffic, including position, identity, intent, and other data (aircraft and vehicles). SAMM is intended to supplement the crew's out-the-window scan and provide real-time cockpit information during taxi, takeoff, and approach to landing. SAMM was developed in accordance with safety recommendations issued by the Runway Joint Safety Implementation Team (JSIT) and Commercial Aviation Safety Team (CAST). SafeRoute airborne applications include Merging & Spacing (M&S) and CDTI Assisted Visual Separation (CAVS). M&S is intended to help maintain spacing between aircraft pairs based on a selected time interval. CAVS provides a means of ensuring separation using distance and differential ground speed from designated traffic.

The CDTI application, developed under an alliance with Astronautics Corporation of America, displays ownship and traffic information provided by SAMM on an airport surface moving map, with the intent of providing flight crew situational awareness to potentially hazardous situations. The CDTI provides traffic when installed with the ACSS SAMM function. Without SAMM, the CDTI will provide a surface moving map, including ownship position when integrated with onboard GPS.

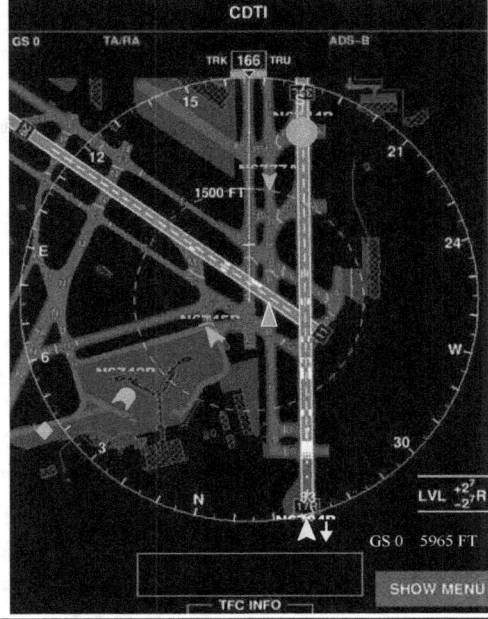

Photo courtesy of  **ACSS**

ACSS	Location: Phoenix, AZ
Hardware Platform	The SAMM function resides on the ACSS TCAS Surveillance Processor, or can be adapted to reside on other avionics platforms. The CDTI may operate on a Class 2 or 3 EFB and can be adopted to operate on an Electronic Flight Instrument System (EFIS), Navigation Display (ND), or Multiple Function Display (MFD).
Display Size	Varies depending on the display platform
Data Format	☐ Raster ☐ Vector ☒ Database *Format* ☒ ARINC Specification 816 *Standards* ☒ RTCA DO-200A ☒ RTCA DO-272: supplier of AMMD to comply *Other:* Varies depending on the avionics and/or display platform
Update Rate	Varies depending on the hardware platform

Airport Information Elements Depicted

Runways	Dark grey with a white border
Runway centerlines	White dashed lines
Runway labels	Blue text in black text boxes
Taxiways	Dark grey
Taxiway centerlines	--
Taxiway labels	Blue
Hold lines	Yellow
Non-movement areas	Black
Ramp areas	Dark grey
Grassy areas	Black
Buildings	Brown border with cross-hatched fill
Building labels	--
Other	

Functions Supported

Ownship Depiction	Yes, Ownship is supported and presented by both SAMM and the CDTI. It is depicted as a magenta triangle. Ownship aircraft provides the flight crew a graphical representation of own aircraft position relative to position of surrounding traffic within the display range. Ownship aircraft symbol is displayed in the middle of the screen when the full compass mode and on the bottom third of the screen when in the arc mode.
Indicators	
Conditions	Prioritization of SAMM-related information with other cockpit information will be evaluated during the upcoming development program.

ACSS	Location: Phoenix, AZ

	Traffic awareness indicators: Visual Indicator in the primary field of view (ADS-B Guidance Display red "TFC" (Traffic) annunciator) as required,

Visual Indicators	and the CDTI depiction of the traffic and airport moving map). In the image below, different categories of traffic are highlighted in yellow and red.
	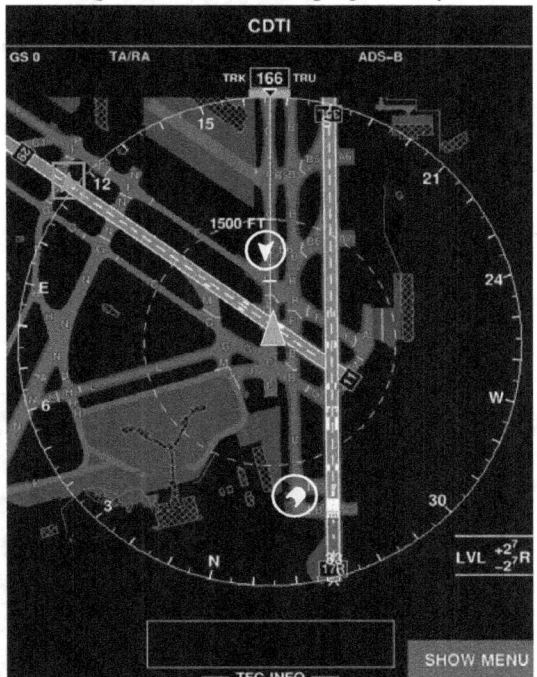
Auditory Indicators	TBD
Decluttering	Yes, a decluttering function is provided • ALL button turns off; TRAFFIC FID, NAV and VECTORS • UNSELECT TGT button cancels the selection (highlight) of the currently active aircraft. No traffic will be selected and the traffic information block in the lower right corner of the CDTI will be blank. Coupled traffic is unaffected. • NO GND TFC button removes the display of all ground traffic (when below 1500 ft RA). • ALL GND TFC button displays all ground traffic (when below 1500 ft RA). 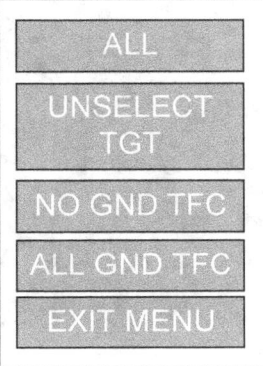

ACSS	Location: Phoenix, AZ
Panning	No panning functionality provided
Traffic Display	SafeRoute™ utilizes Automatic Dependent Surveillance – Broadcast (ADS-B), Traffic Information Service – Broadcast (TIS-B), and Cockpit Display of Traffic Information (CDTI) technology. Traffic is represented on the CDTI using colors and symbols (icons). Note: Figure shows the entire symbol set that was reviewed with the FAA. The color philosophy used for the traffic symbols is defined as follows: • Magenta – Ownship symbol • Cyan – Airborne traffic • Green – Coupled traffic (and related text) • Amber – Category 1 Traffic indicates a potentially hazardous situation • Red – Category 2 Traffic indicates a high risk of a hazardous situation • Light Brown/Tan – Ground traffic • Grey – Circular background to a traffic symbol to indicate selected traffic In general the symbol or icon indicates the performance characteristics of the ADS-B data being reported by the corresponding traffic. 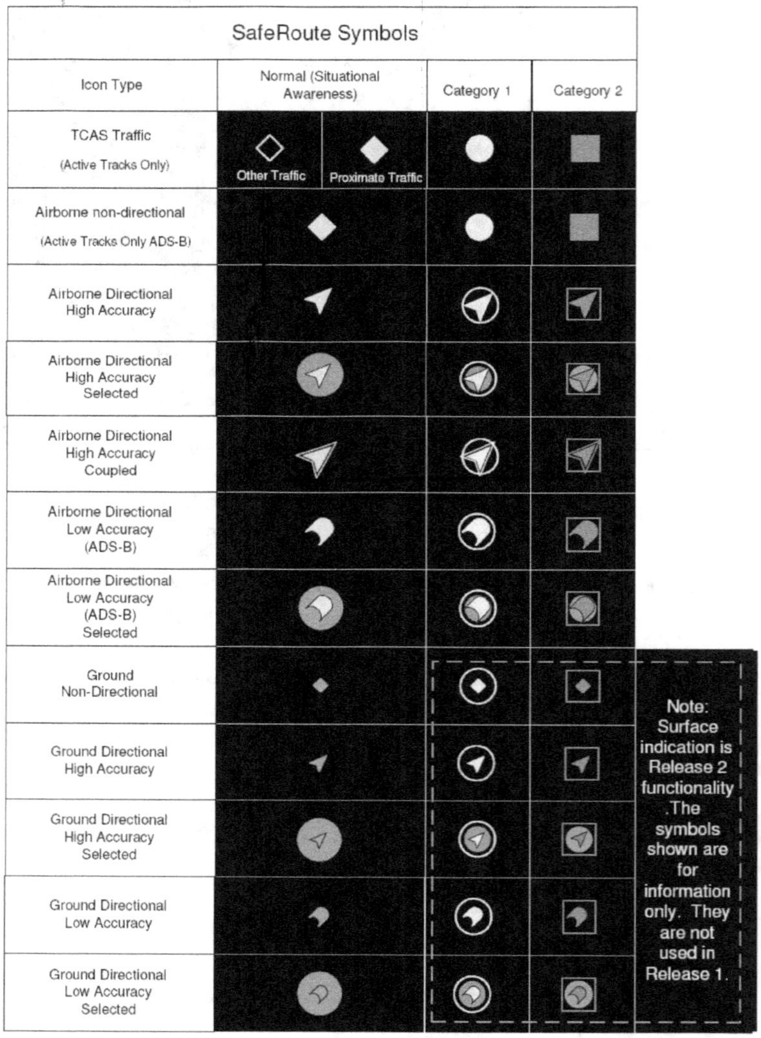

28

ACSS	Location: Phoenix, AZ
Route Guidance	Runway Awareness Application The Runway Awareness application is designed to provide the flight crew with take-off or landing runway situational awareness relative to ownship position. The flight crew will be able to enter the runway identifier into the EFB or other crew interface device resulting in colored highlights of the desired runway. See picture below. 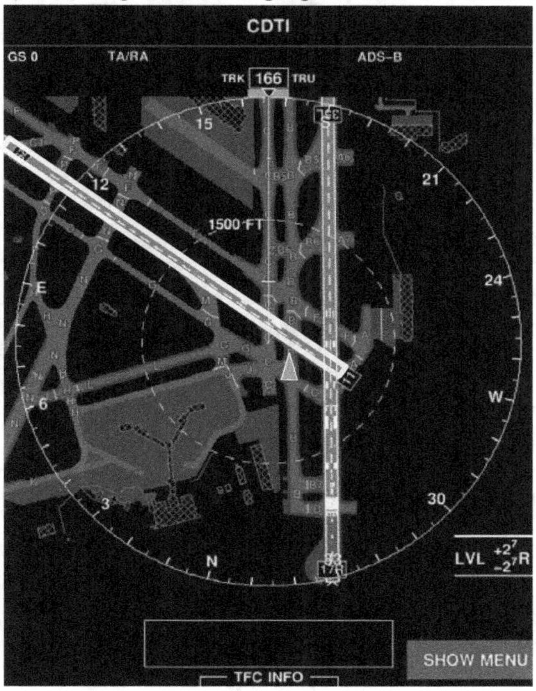
Zooming/Autozoom	Yes, zooming capability is provided, not autozoom The + and – Zoom Keys increase and decrease the CDTI zoom level.

FlightPrep		**Location:**	Aurora, OR
Product(s)	ChartCase Professional, ChartCase Express		
Website(s)	www.flightprep.com		
Approvals / Compliance	*Avionics Box Type* : ☐ Installed/MFD ☒ EFB (Class ☒ 1 ☒ 2 ☐ 3) *Authority*: ☒ FAA ☐ EASA ☐ Other *Type of Approval/Compliance* TSO: ☐ C113 ☐ C165 ☐ C166A ☐ Other AC: ☐ AC 20-159 ☒ AC120-76A ☐ TC ☐ STC *Aircraft*: _____ ☐ Order 8900.1 ☐ RTCA DO-178B (Level ___) *Other Notes*: EFB software compliant with AC 91-78, FAA Notice N8900.17		

Product Overview

ChartCase Professional™ is moving map software that provides a surface application using geo-referenced electronic charts. Ownship position from GPS data can be presented on these charts. In addition to the airport diagrams, ChartCase Professional™ includes all Sectional Charts, WAC Charts, High/Low Enroute Charts, Instrument Procedures, Airport Diagrams, TAC and vector charts for the U.S. The software can be used on most Windows-based computers.

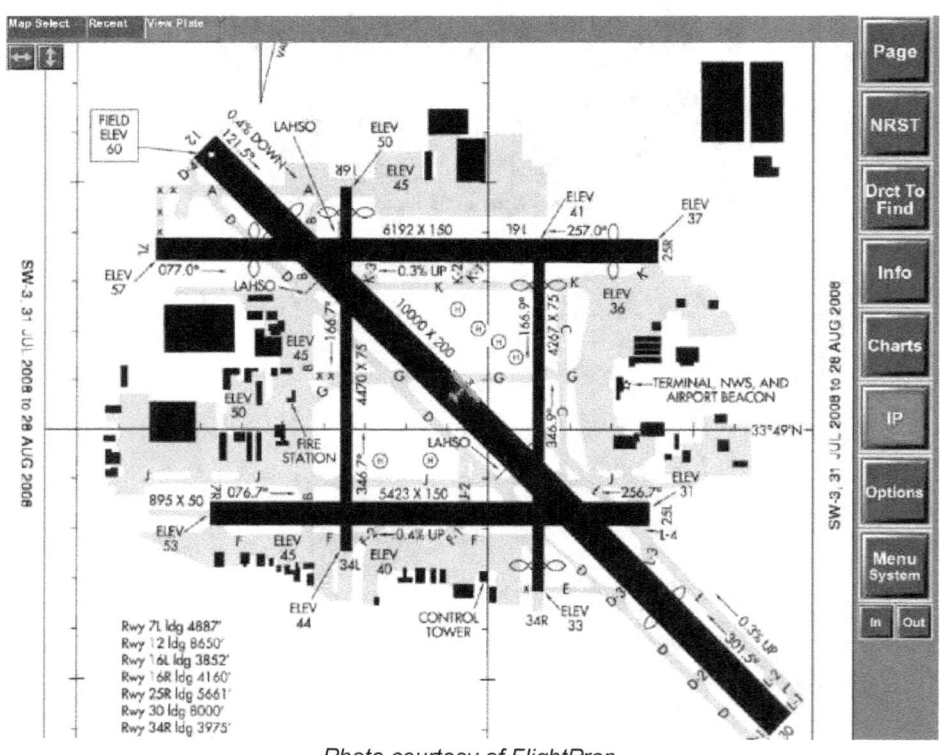

Photo courtesy of FlightPrep.

Hardware Platform	EFB/Tablet PC Class 1 & 2
Display Size	From 7" WVGA (640 X 480) to 60" monitor and beyond

FlightPrep		Location:	Aurora, OR
Data Format	☒ Raster ☒ Vector ☐ Database *Format* ☐ ARINC Specification 816 *Standards* ☐ RTCA DO-200A ☐ RTCA DO-272		
Update Rate	Determined by hardware and GPS. Usually 1 – 3 times per sec.		
Airport Information Elements Depicted			
Runways	Black		
Runway centerlines	--		
Runway labels	Black		
Taxiways	Grey		
Taxiway centerlines	--		
Taxiway labels	Black		
Hold lines	--		
Non-movement areas	White		
Ramp areas	Grey		
Grassy areas	White		
Buildings	Black		
Building labels	Black		
Other			
Functions Supported			
Ownship Depiction	Yes, there are a variety of different icons available to depict position. There is also the ability to adjust the transparency of the icon and to make it completely invisible for a moving map without own ship position. 		
Indicators	Indicators provided in the software are for alerting that GPS signal has been lost or if the system is engaged in a Simulator Mode		
Conditions	No GPS Connected, Simulator Mode		
Visual Indicators	Red Message block for loss of GPS Signal, Yellow message block for Simulator Mode		
Auditory Indicators	None		
Decluttering	Not Available on Raster Charts, Available on Vector based charts		
Panning	Yes		
Traffic Display	No		
Route Guidance	No		
Zooming/Autozoom	Zoom		

Garmin		**Location:**	Olathe, KS

Product(s)	SafeTaxi
Website(s)	www.garmin.com
Approvals / Compliance	*Avionics Box Type* : ☒ Installed/MFD ☐ EFB (Class ☐ 1 ☐ 2 ☐ 3) *Authority*: ☒ FAA ☒ EASA ☐ Other *Type of Approval/Compliance* TSO: ☒ C113 (and EASA equivalent) ☐ C165 ☐ C166A ☐ Other AC: ☐ AC 20-159 ☐ AC120-76A ☐ TC ☐ STC *Aircraft*: _____ ☐ Order 8900.1 ☒ RTCA DO-178B (Level _D_) *Other Notes* SafeTaxi is available on portable devices (GPS 696)

Product Overview

SafeTaxi provides ownship position on database-driven airport diagrams. SafeTaxi is offered as a function on Garmin's portable 496 and their integrated glass cockpit systems (e.g., G600, G900X and G1000). Two electronic chart functions are also offered. ChartView provides access to geo-referenced airport charts and instrument approach plates provided by Jeppesen. FliteCharts provides an electronic version of National Aeronautical Chart Office (NACO) approach charts and airport diagrams, Departure Procedures (DP), and Standard Terminal Arrival Routes (STARs); these charts are not geo-referenced and therefore can not show ownship position.

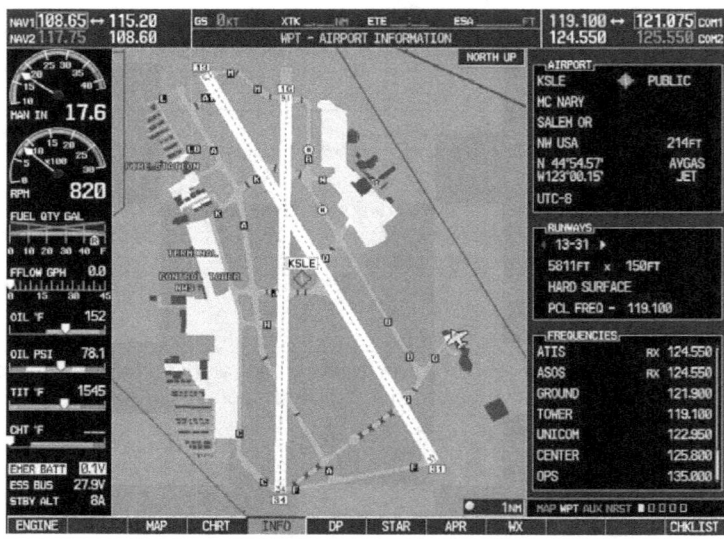

Photo courtesy of Garmin.

Hardware Platform	Integrated system (G1000, G600, G900X, G1000 for King Air C90) Panel mount (GMX 200) Portable (GPSMAP 495 & 496)
Display Size	Varies depending on the hardware system
Data Format	☐ Raster ☐ Vector ☒ Database *Format* ☐ ARINC Specification 816 *Standards* ☒ RTCA DO-200A ☐ RTCA DO-272

Garmin	Location: Olathe, KS
Update Rate	5 Hz
Airport Information Elements Depicted	
Runways	White
Runway centerlines	Grey dotted lines
Runway labels	White text in black text boxes
Taxiways	Grey
Taxiway centerlines	--
Taxiway labels	White text in black text boxes
Hold lines	--
Non-movement areas	Green
Ramp areas	Grey
Grassy areas	Green
Buildings	Black
Building labels	Black text
Other	
Functions Supported	
Ownship Depiction	Yes. Ownship is depicted with an airplane icon.
Indicators	Hot spots embedded; circled in magenta
Conditions	--
Visual Indicators	--
Auditory Indicators	--
Decluttering	Yes; Decluttering is tied to map range/scale so that features are removed as the map is zoomed out and added as the map is zoomed in
Panning	Yes

Traffic Display	SafeTaxi supports display of ADS-B, TIS-B, and TCAS traffic using the following symbols:

Garmin G1000-Series Traffic (TFC) Symbols

Non-Directional Traffic Symbols (TIS, TAS, ADS-B)		Directional Traffic Symbols (ADS-B)	
○	Traffic Advisory (TA), inside display range	▷	Traffic Advisory (TA), inside display range
◒	Traffic Advisory (TA), outside display range	◓	Traffic Advisory (TA), outside display range
◇	Proximate Advisory (PA)	▷	Proximate Advisory (PA)
◆	Other Traffic (Note 1)	▶	Other Traffic (Note 1)
◆	Degraded Positional Accuracy or Degraded Integrity (Note 1, Note 2)	⊃	Degraded Positional Accuracy or Degraded Integrity (Note 2)
◇	Non-Directional TFC on Ground	▷	Directional TFC on Ground
▢	Ground Vehicle	▢	Ground Vehicle

Note 1: For possible future use.

Note 2: For all current Garmin implementations, a degraded target is valid only for Traffic Situational Awareness and as an aid to visual acquisition of the traffic. The "degraded" status, based on an assessment of inadequate accuracy or integrity, indicates that this target may not be selected and may not be used for other applications.

Garmin MX 20, GMX 200 Traffic (TFC) Symbols

Non-Directional Traffic		Directional Traffic	
○	Non-Directional Caution TFC	⟶	Directional Caution TFC
◒	Caution TFC Outside Display Range	◓	Caution TFC Outside Display Range
◇	Non-Directional Non-Threat TFC	⟶	Directional Non-Threat TFC
◇	Non-Directional Non-Threat TFC	⊃	Non-Threat TFC, Degraded Pos. or Integrity (See Note)
◆	Non-Directional TFC on Ground	⟶	Directional TFC on Ground
▢	Ground Vehicle	▢	Ground Vehicle

Garmin				Location:	Olathe, KS

Selected Traffic

◇	Non-Directional Selected TFC
▷	Directional Selected TFC

Note: For all current Garmin implementations, a degraded target is valid only for Traffic Situational Awareness and as an aid to visual acquisition of the traffic. The "degraded" status, based on an assessment of inadequate accuracy or integrity, indicates that this target may not be selected and may not be used for any other applications.

Garmin GNS 400 Series and GNS 500 Series TIS Traffic Symbols

○—	Directional Caution TIS TFC
◇—	Directional Proximate TIS TFC
◆—	Directional Other TIS TFC

Note: The GNS400- and GNS500-series displays currently do not fully support ADS-B. If connected to a TIS-capable Mode S transponder, the symbols for TIS targets resemble TCAS symbols, augmented with lines pointing in the approximate direction of motion of the traffic (as given in the TIS uplink from the SSR radar on the ground).

Route Guidance	--
Zooming/Autozoom	Zoom

Honeywell		**Location:** Phoenix, Arizona
Product(s)	SmartRunway SmartRunway is the new name for Runway Awareness and Advisory System (RAAS). SmartRunway supports aural and visual alerts and advisories.	
Website(s)	• www.honeywell.com • Runway Awareness and Advisory System (RAAS)	
Approvals / Compliance	*Avionics Box Type* : ☒ Installed/MFD ☐ EFB (Class ☐ 1 ☐ 2 ☐ 3) *Authority*: ☒ FAA ☐ EASA ☐ Other *Type of Approval/Compliance* TSO: ☐ C113 ☐ C165 ☐ C166A ☒ Other (TSO-C151) AC: ☐ AC 20-159 ☐ AC120-76A ☐ TC ☐ STC *Aircraft*: _____ ☐ Order 8900.1 ☐ RTCA DO-178B (Level ___) *Other Notes*: RAAS is contained within the EGPWS which is TSO'd to TSO-C151	

Product Overview

SmartRunway (Runway Awareness and Advisory System – RAAS) is a low cost solution which is intended to help mitigate the risk of runway incursion accidents and incidents. It utilizes GPS and the world-wide database of airports and runways within the EGPWS. This runway-based detection and alerting capability is the foundation for new surface moving map and alerting products currently in the pipeline. SmartRunway supports aural and visual alerts and advisories.

Hardware Platform	SmartRunway (RAAS) is a software application that is hosted within the MK V and MK VII EGPWS and the Primus Epic integrated avionics systems.
Display Size	Various
Data Format	☐ Raster ☐ Vector ☒ Database *Format* ☐ ARINC Specification 816 *Standards* ☐ RTCA DO-200A ☐ RTCA DO-272
Update Rate	--

Functions Supported

Ownship Depiction	SmartRunway (RAAS) does not support an ownship display.
Indicators	SmartRunway (Runway Awareness and Advisory System – RAAS) utilizes aural and visual alerts and advisories. Visual messages are displayed on existing displays in the same space where terrain is displayed (e.g. Navigation Display, Weather Radar Indicator)
Auditory Indicators	Approaching runway – in air advisory • "Approaching" followed by the runway identifier, e.g., "*Approaching Two-Five-Right*". • Threshold for presentation: aircraft is between 750 feet and 300 feet above the airport elevation (AFE); aircraft is within approximately 3 nautical miles of the runway; aircraft track is aligned with the runway within 20 degrees; and aircraft position is within approximately 200 feet, plus runway width, of the runway centerline. • Advisory suppressed between 550 feet and 450 feet above runway elevation

Approaching runway – on ground advisory

- "Approaching" followed by the runway identifier, e.g., "*Approaching Three-Four-Left*".
- Threshold for presentation: aircraft ground speed is less than 40 knots; and aircraft is within a specified distance from the runway. (Distance is a function of aircraft ground speed and closure angle with the runway, such that a higher ground speed would require an earlier advisory).

Distance Remaining – Landing And Roll-Out Advisory

- For systems using feet as the unit of length, the advisories are generated at whole thousand-foot intervals, with the last possible advisory at 500 feet. For example, a RAAS equipped aircraft landing on a 9000 foot runway, with the Distance Remaining advisory issued starting at 2000 feet from the runway end, would generate the following advisories: "*Two-Thousand Remaining*", "*One-Thousand Remaining*", and "*Five-Hundred Remaining*".
- For systems using meters as the unit of length, the advisories are generated at multiples of 300-metre intervals, with the last possible advisory occurs at 100 meters. For example, a RAAS equipped aircraft landing on a 3000 meter runway, with the Distance Remaining advisory issued starting at 900 meters from the runway end, would generate the following advisories: "*Nine-Hundred Remaining*", "*Six-Hundred Remaining*", "*Three-Hundred Remaining*", and "*One-Hundred Remaining*".
- Threshold for presentation:
  - Aircraft is within 100 feet of the ground, over the last half of the runway or a specified distance from the runway end; or
  - Aircraft is on the ground, on the last half of the runway (default) or a specified distance from the runway end; and aircraft ground speed is above 40 knots
- Advisories are inhibited once the aircraft climbs above 100 feet Radio Altitude or aircraft climb rate is greater than 450 fpm.

Runway End Advisory

- "*One-Hundred Remaining*" for units of feet and "*Thirty Remaining*" for units of meters.
- Threshold for presentation: aircraft is on a runway and aligned within 20 degrees of runway heading; aircraft approaches within 100 feet of the runway end; and aircraft ground speed is below 40 Knots.

Approaching Short Runway – In Air Advisory

- The Approaching Runway Advisory is appended with available runway length information, e.g., "Approaching Two-Five-Left, Three-Thousand-Eight-Hundred-Available".
- All conditions for approaching In-Air Advisory are satisfied; and the aligned runway is shorter than a nominal runway length.

Insufficient runway length – on-ground advisory

- Runway length remaining information is appended to the routine "*On Runway*" advisory, e.g., "*On Runway Three-Four-Left, Two-Thousand Remaining*". The source for the runway distance remaining is the EGPWS runway database to the nearest 100 feet (100 meters).
- Threshold for presentation: all conditions for a routine On-Runway Advisory are satisfied; and available distance for takeoff is less than the defined nominal runway length.

	Extended holding on runway advisory
	• After a specified time period, an aural advisory consisting of the message "On Runway" followed by the runway identifier is generated and annunciated twice for each time interval. For example, if an aircraft is cleared to line-up-and-wait on runway 22 and, after waiting in position for an extended period, the system will annunciate "On Runway Two-Two, On Runway Two-Two".
	• Threshold for presentation: aircraft enters a runway; aircraft heading is within 20 degrees of runway heading; and aircraft along-track distance does not change more than 100 ft in a period of time considered to be an extended holding period (the time period can be configured for 60, 90, 120, 180, 240, or 300 seconds).
	Taxiway take-off advisory
	• "On *Taxiway! On Taxiway!*"
	• Threshold for presentation: Ground speed of the aircraft exceeds 40 knots; and aircraft is on a surface other than a runway.
	Distance remaining – rejected take-off advisory
	• For systems using feet as the unit of length, the advisories are generated at whole thousand-foot intervals, with the last possible advisory occurring at 500 feet. For example, a RAAS equipped aircraft aborting a takeoff on a 9000 foot runway, with the Distance Remaining advisory issued starting at 2000 feet, would generate the following advisories: "Two-Thousand Remaining", "One-Thousand Remaining", and "Five-Hundred Remaining".
	• For systems using meters as the unit of length, the advisories are generated at multiples of 300-metre intervals, with the last possible advisory occurring at 100 meters. For example, a RAAS equipped aircraft aborting a takeoff on a 3000 meter runway, with the Distance Remaining advisory issued starting at 600 meters, would generate the following advisories: "Six-Hundred Remaining", "Three-Hundred Remaining", and "One- Hundred Remaining".
	• Threshold for presentation: Aircraft is on a runway; ground speed is greater than 40 knots; aircraft ground speed during the take-off roll decreases by 7 knots from its maximum; and aircraft is on the last half of the runway (default) or a specified distance from the runway end.
	• Advisories terminate when the ground speed decreases below 40 knots.
	Taxiway Landing Alert
	• "Caution *Taxiway! Caution Taxiway!*"
	• Threshold for presentation: Aircraft is airborne and within the vertical limits, and the aircraft is not aligned with a runway
Decluttering	Decluttering of audio and visual alerts is performed internal to the EGPWS.
Panning	N/A
Traffic Display	All EGPWS visuals can be overlayed by Traffic displays.
Route Guidance	Route guidance is not provided, although SmartRunway (RAAS) can be used to confirm the route along the way.
Zooming/Autozoom	N/A

Jeppesen Product 1 of 2 (Airport Moving Map for EFB)   Location: Englewood, CO

Product(s)	Jeppesen Airport Moving Map software and database for EFB systems
Website(s)	• www.jeppesen.com • http://www.jeppesen.com/wlcs/index.jsp?section=ca&content=efb_mm.jsp
Approvals / Compliance	*Avionics Box Type* : ☐ Installed/MFD ☒ EFB (Class ☐ 1 ☒ 2 ☒ 3) *Authority:* ☒ FAA ☐ EASA ☐ Other *Type of Approval/Compliance* TSO: ☐ C113 ☒ C165 ☐ C166A ☐ Other AC: ☒ AC 20-159 ☒ AC120-76A ☐ TC ☐ STC *Aircraft*: _____ ☒ Order 8900.1 ☒ RTCA DO-178B (Level _D_) *Other Notes*: • Airport Moving Map for Jeppesen **Class 2** EFB systems: Awarded FAA TSO Authorization March, 2008 according to AC 20-159, 120-76A, TSO C-165 • Airport Moving Map for Boeing **Class 3** EFB systems: Approved and in use since October, 2003 according to AC 120-76A (Type C)

Product Overview

Jeppesen Airport Moving Map (AMM) for EFB renders high-resolution Jeppesen airport database maps, including runways, taxiways, ramps, structures, and movement control features. With GPS, the application depicts ownship position in both north-up and track-up (moving map) orientation. AMM entered service on Boeing Class 3 EFB in 2003. In 2008, Jeppesen was granted FAA TSO Authorization for use on Class 2 EFBs. The Class 2 software is designed to work on Windows-based EFBs that meet reasonable minimum system requirements. Jeppesen provides airport databases through subscription. Airport Moving Map is part of a suite of Jeppesen applications offered for EFBs.

Note: Jeppesen Airport Moving Map is designed to provide supplemental position awareness during taxi operations. It is a supplement to Jeppesen electronic charting solutions available for EFB. For a full description of Jeppesen EFB charting solutions, refer to the Volpe Industry Review for EFB.

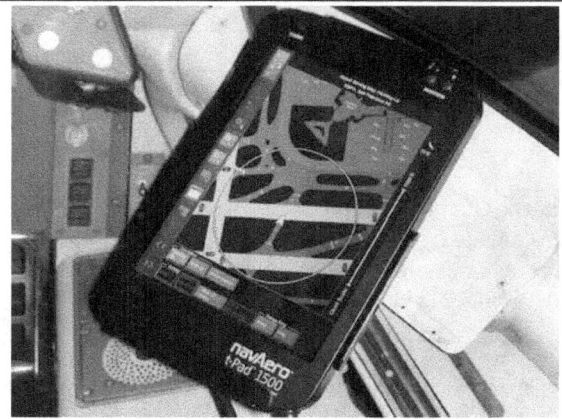 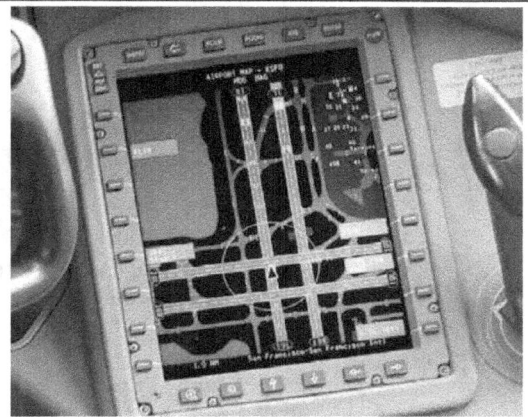

L: Jeppesen Airport Moving Map (AMM) on Class 2 EFB.   R: Jeppesen AMM on Boeing Class 3 EFB.
Shown by permission from Jeppesen

Hardware Platform	AMM is a software and database solution designed to run on Class 2 and 3 EFB hardware platforms that meet minimum system requirements.
Display Size	AMM operates on displays of various sizes and resolutions, in both portrait and landscape orientations.

Jeppesen Product 1 of 2 (Airport Moving Map for EFB)   Location: Englewood, CO

Database Format	☐ Raster ☐ Vector ☒ Database *Format* ☐ ARINC Specification 816 *Standards* ☒ RTCA DO-200A (for Accuracy, Integrity, Resolution, Traceability, Timeliness, Completeness, and Format) ☒ RTCA DO-272 *Other:* FAA Letter of Acceptance (LoA), February, 2009. Overall accuracy is guaranteed 5 meters or better.
Update Rate	N/A. This is a software and database product.
Airport Information Elements Depicted	
Runways	Light grey All runway markings visible from the satellite are depicted in white to match real-world paint markings.
Runway centerlines	White runway paint markings, including runway centerlines, are depicted as seen in the real world.
Runway labels	Blue text in blue oval with black background. For runways visible in the view, the runway labels are always displayed at view edge, regardless of zoom and pan setting. Closed Runways are labeled with Amber text in Amber oval with black background. An Amber X marks the runways and runway labels. Closed Displaced Runway Threshold: Same fill color as the runway, but with Amber outline and Amber X marks on both ends of the Displaced Threshold.
Taxiways	Dark grey
Taxiway centerlines	Not shown.
Taxiway labels	White characters
Hold lines	Amber
Non-movement areas	Dirt and grass areas shown in black. Blast pads and overrun areas shown in light grey.
Ramp areas	Dark grey
Grassy areas	Black
Buildings	Blue
Building labels	White text
Other	Closed Ramp, Taxiway, Parking Stand areas: Black fill with red outline. Areas Under Construction: Bounded by a red border. Other vertical structures such as trees are shown in blue just like buildings. Airport Beacons are shown as a green star within a green circle on black background.
Functions Supported	
Ownship Depiction	 Ownship is indicated (amber chevron Class 2, isosceles triangle Class 3).
Indicators	Airport Moving Map is designed to provide supplemental position information on EFBs.

Jeppesen Product 1 of 2 (Airport Moving Map for EFB)	Location: Englewood, CO
Conditions	N/A
Visual Indicators	Constant ownship position updating while on the ground at an airport in the database, as long as healthy position data is received from the system.
Auditory Indicators	N/A
Decluttering	Labels are always presented in read-right manner and are automatically de-cluttered to prevent label collisions and overprints. Appropriate label detail is provided at each zoom level, for example runway identifiers and key taxiway identifiers are always shown. As the AMM is zoomed in, additional labels are added, showing more detail such as concourse and gate identifiers.
Panning	Panning is supported when displaying the map in north-up orientation.
Traffic Display	Other traffic is not displayed.
Route Guidance	Route guidance is not displayed.
Zooming/Autozoom	Zooming function is provided in both north-up and track-up orientations.

Jeppesen Product 2 of 2 (JeppView)

Location: Englewood, CO

Product(s)	JeppView (FliteDeck and MFD)
Website(s)	www.jeppesen.com
Approvals	Responsibility of the end user.

Product Overview

JeppView is a suite of applications that provide electronic aeronautical charts for both ground-based and in flight use. The JeppView charts provide the same coverage as Jeppesen's Airway Manuals. JeppView can be used on desktop, laptop, and tablet computers. JeppView FliteDeck is the Jeppesen software adapted for use in flight. JeppView MFD is a chart solution designed for integration into avionics-built multi-function displays, using software developed by the MFD provider. Ownship position can be depicted on the geo-referenced Jeppesen charts, if the aircraft is equipped with a GPS signal that is integrated into the display device. Jeppesen does not provide the actual physical displays; this is a software product and database service.

Note: This product family utilizes standard Jeppesen airport diagrams from the chart database for the surface moving map function. Database source, resolution and functionality are not the same as EFB Airport Moving Map (AMM), described in Jeppesen product 1 of 2.

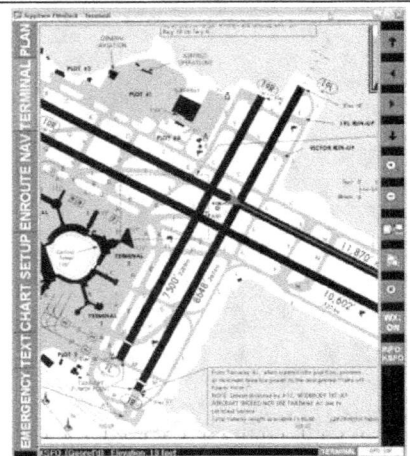 

L: JeppView FliteDeck for generic PC platforms.   **R:** JeppView MFD Example (shown: Avidyne EX5000)

Shown by permission from Jeppesen.

Hardware Platform	JeppView FliteDeck: Desktop, laptop, tablet computers that meet minimum system requirements. JeppView MFD for avionics systems: Various MFDs from Avidyne (EX500, EX5000, ADX210, ADX212, Entegra Release 9), Garmin (G1000, G900X, G600, GMX200, MX20), Honeywell (Primus Epic Inav), Rockwell Collins (Proline), and Universal Avionics (UCD).
Display Size	JeppView FliteDeck: Displays of various sizes, orientations, and resolutions in both portrait and landscape orientations. JeppView MFD: Displays of various sizes, orientations, and resolutions as developed by the avionics manufacturers.
Data Format	☐ Raster ☒ Vector ☐ Database *Format* ☐ ARINC Specification 816 *Standards* ☐ RTCA DO-200A ☐ RTCA DO-272 *Other:* The diagrams are static and pre-composed, so read-right text only supports North up mode.
Update Rate	N/A. This is a software and database product.

Jeppesen Product 2 of 2 (JeppView)	Location: Englewood, CO

Airport Information Elements Depicted

Runways	Black
Runway centerlines	N/A
Runway labels	Black
Taxiways	Grey
Taxiway centerlines	N/A
Taxiway labels	Black
Hold lines	N/A
Non-movement areas	White
Ramp areas	Grey
Grassy areas	White
Buildings	Black
Building labels	Black text
Other	Various additional airport diagram markings and procedural notes.

Functions Supported

Ownship Depiction	 JeppView FliteDeck: Green chevron (shown). JeppView MFD: Varies depending on the manufacturer.
Indicators	N/A
Conditions	N/A
Visual Indicators	Constant ownship position updating while on the ground at an airport in the database, as long as healthy position data is received from the system.
Auditory Indicators	N/A
Decluttering	N/A, charts are pre-composed static north-up images.
Panning	Yes
Traffic Display	N/A
Route Guidance	N/A
Zooming/Autozoom	Yes

Lufthansa Systems		**Location:** Frankfurt, Germany
Product(s)	Lido Airport Moving Map	
Website(s)	www.lhsystems.com	
Approvals / Compliance	*Avionics Box Type :* ☐ Installed/MFD ☒ EFB (Class ☐ 1 ☒ 2 ☒ 3) *Authority:* ☒ FAA ☒ EASA ☐ Other *Type of Approval/Compliance* – In progress TSO: ☐ C113 ☒ C165 ☐ C166A ☐ Other AC: ☒ AC 20-159 ☒ AC120-76A ☐ TC ☐ STC *Aircraft*: _____ ☒ Order 8900.1 ☒ RTCA DO-178B (Level D)	

Product Overview

Lido Airport Moving Map is intended to act as a runway incursion prevention system as well as airport information system. It replaces the (paper/static) ground chart and shows a dynamic ground chart using the Lido RouteManual charting standard. Own-ship position (north up or track up) is superimposed on the chart; the application is fully integrated into the Lido eRouteManual electronic charting solution.

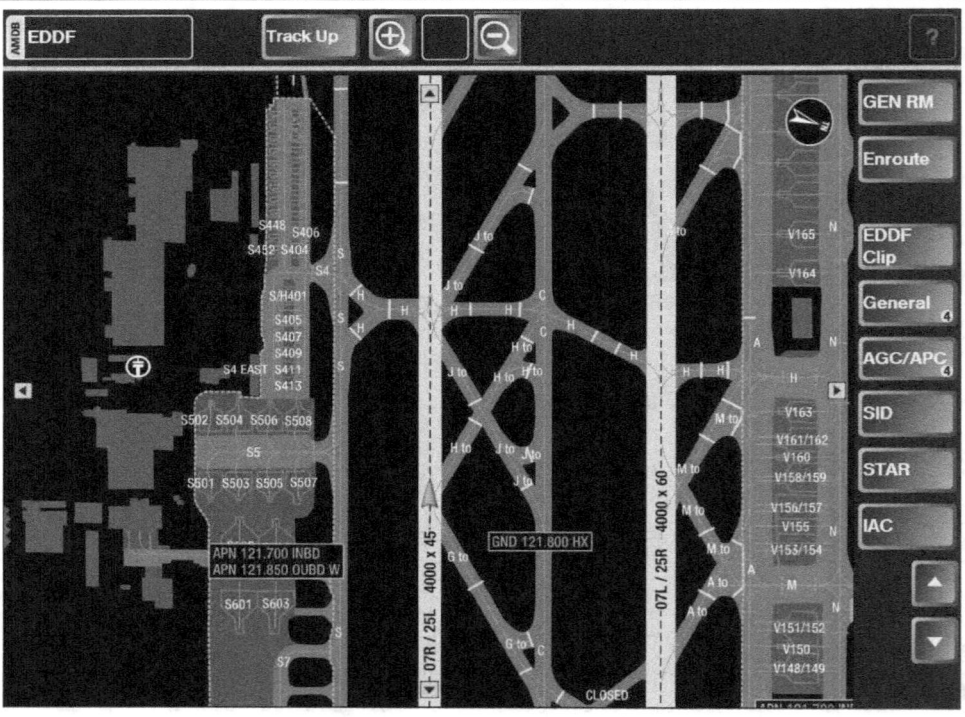

Photo provided courtesy of Lido. Research Display Only.

Hardware Platform	EFB Class 1-3 (Class 1 without own-ship position)
Display Size	Any
Data Format	☐ Raster ☐ Vector ☒ Database *Standards* ☒ ARINC Specification 816 ☒ RTCA DO-200A ☒ RTCA DO-272 *Other:* Lido proprietary format
Update Rate	Acc. RTCA DO-272

Lufthansa Systems

Location: Frankfurt, Germany

Airport Information Elements Depicted

The method of depiction shown in the photo and described below reflects the night mode implementation, according to the Lido RouteManual charting standard.

Runways	Light grey
Runway centerlines	Black dashed line
Runway labels	Deconflicted black text aligned to runway
Taxiways	Grey shape
Taxiway centerlines	Yellow line
Taxiway labels	Deconflicted white horizontal text
Hold lines	Yellow line
Non-movement areas	--
Ramp areas	Grey
Grassy areas	--
Buildings	Brown
Building labels	Deconflicted white horizontal text
Other	According Lido RouteManual charting standard

Functions Supported

Ownship Depiction	Yes, orange chevron (look/color subject to change)
Indicators	Runway ahead warning; graphical NOTAM integration
Conditions	N/A
Visual Indicators	Runway ahead warning by overlay message with red outline and adding red outline to runway (color/style subject to change). Screenshot in day mode.
Auditory Indicators	N/A
Decluttering	Yes, zooming in further shows more detail, like taxiway lines, labels, etc.
Panning	Yes (Plan Mode)
Traffic Display	No
Route Guidance	Colored line along taxi route. Route entered graphically or textually. Route could also be loaded from file (company routes) or any interface. NOTAMs to be interpreted and displayed, e.g. as restriction or closed taxiway.
Zooming/Autozoom	Yes

MAPTECH Aeronautical Data	Location: Exeter, NH
Product(s)	GENESYS SMM
Website(s)	• www.maptechaero.com • Distributed by DAC International www.dacint.com
Approvals / Compliance	*Avionics Box Type* : ☐ Installed/MFD ☒ EFB (Class ☐ 1 ☒ 2 ☒ 3) *Authority*: ☒ FAA ☐ EASA ☐ Other *Type of Approval/Compliance* TSO: ☒ C113 ☒ C165 ☒ C166A ☐ Other *Notes*: • FAA TSO C165 in process for August 2009. • FAA TSO C166A in process for September 2009. AC: ☒ AC 20-159 ☒ AC120-76A ☐ TC ☒ STC *Aircraft*: CRJ, ERJ, DHC-8, B767, C130, L382, DC-8, B737, B777, Hawker/Beechcraft ☒ Order 8900.1 ☒ RTCA DO-178B (Level _C_)

Product Overview

The GENESYS SMM is a software application available as an add-on to the MAPTECH GENESYS suite

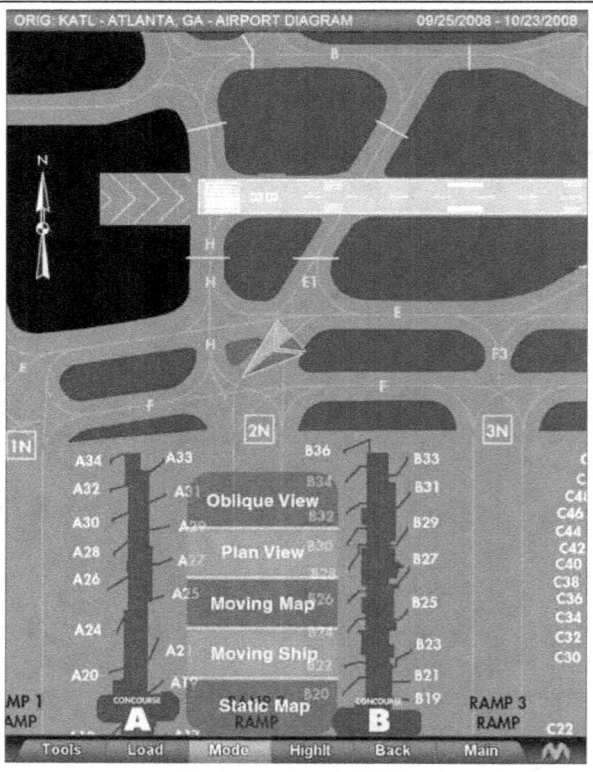

Photo courtesy of DAC.

Hardware Platform	GENESYS SMM is designed for use on a Class 2 or Class 3 EFB or Multi-function Flight Information Display Unit (MFIDU).
Display Size	8.4", 10.4", 12.1"

MAPTECH Aeronautical Data	Location: Exeter, NH
Data Format	☒ Raster ☒ Vector ☒ Database *Format* ☐ ARINC Specification 816 *Standards* ☒ RTCA DO-200A ☒ RTCA DO-272 *Other:* Both raster and vector technologies are utilized to maximize the benefits of each format. Submeter accuracy satellite imagery is used to meet or exceed the accuracy requirements of RTCA DO-272.
Update Rate	Installation Specific, approximately 1-10 Hz dependent on source inputs

Airport Information Elements Depicted

Runways	Light gray
Runway centerlines	White
Runway labels	White
Taxiways	Dark gray
Taxiway centerlines	Yellow
Taxiway labels	White
Hold lines	Yellow
Non-movement areas	Black
Ramp areas	Light gray
Grassy areas	Green
Buildings	Brown
Building labels	White
Other	

Functions Supported

Ownship Depiction	Administrator selectable icons/colors A green triangle is depicted in the image.
Indicators	Active runway marking
Conditions	Pilots enter runway information during preflight of the EFB, and this information is picked up by the surface moving map application
Visual Indicators	A magenta box is drawn around the active runway
Auditory Indicators	None
Decluttering	None
Panning	Yes
Traffic Display	None
Route Guidance	Manual taxi highlighting available
Zooming/Autozoom	Yes

Rockwell-Collins, Inc.		Location: Cedar Rapids, IA
Product(s)	A moving map implementation displaying airport surface, ownship, traffic, and runway related indications and traffic conflict alerts, supporting A-SMGCS (Advanced Surface Movement Guidance and Control System). Additionally, taxi route, taxi clearance limit, route deviation alert and clearance deviation alert are available (if taxi route and clearance limit information is made available).	
Website(s)	www.rockwellcollins.com	
Approvals / Compliance	*Avionics Box Type* : ☐ Installed/MFD ☒ EFB (Class ☐ 1 ☒ 2 ☐ 3) *Authority*: ☐ FAA ☐ EASA ☒ Other (Swedish CAA) *Type of Approval/Compliance* TSO: ☐ C113 ☐ C165 ☐ C166A ☐ Other AC: ☐ AC 20-159 ☐ AC120-76A ☐ TC ☒ STC *Aircraft*: __Boeing 737NG__ ☐ Order 8900.1 ☒ RTCA DO-178B (Level _D_) *Note*: The software is designed to meet the requirements of RTCA DO-178B but it is not approved.	

Product Overview

Rockwell Collins worked with LFV, SAS, Avtech, Boeing, Delft University, and EUROCONTROL to research, develop, and evaluate a surface moving map implementation of advanced concepts for all aircraft categories. This work was performed for the Northern European ADS-B Network Update-Program II+. The implementation shows current Rockwell Collins capability and provides a platform and framework for future development. The system behaves as a basic Cockpit Display of Traffic Information (CDTI), displaying ownship and ADS-B traffic information graphically, on the ground and in the air. The system has the capability to receive data-linked taxi route instructions (including clearance information), display them graphically on the airport surface map, and provide clearance and route conformance monitoring. The system is installed on SAS Boeing 737NG aircraft for operational evaluation on commercial revenue flights. The taxi route data link provision was implemented specifically for Arlanda airport, Stockholm, Sweden.

Rockwell Collins also provides a surface map application based on electronic airport diagrams using a Jeppesen airport surface database for aircraft Adaptive Flight Displays (AFD). The IFIS product (not shown here) currently provides airport moving map with ownship position on a forward display.

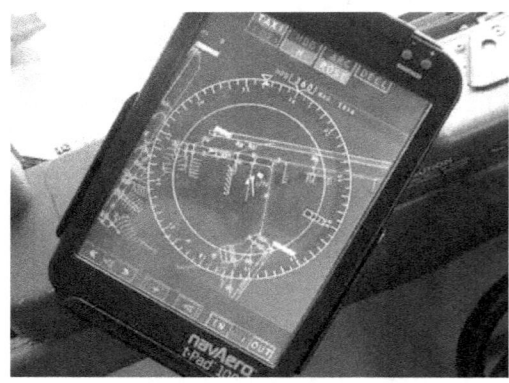

Photo courtesy of Rockwell Collins.

Hardware Platform	The application is currently running on the NavAero t-Pad 1000 with a touchscreen, but it was originally built for the BF Goodrich EFB with bezel keys. It can be hosted on similar EFBs (either class 2 or class 3).
Display Size	The NavAero t-Pad 1000 is a 10.4" TFT LCD display with touchscreen used in portrait mode with a resolution of 768x1024.

Rockwell-Collins, Inc.			**Location:** Cedar Rapids, IA	

Data Format	☐ Raster ☐ Vector ☒ Database *Format* ☐ ARINC Specification 816 *Standards* ☐ RTCA DO-200A ☐ RTCA DO-272 *Other:* Using custom airport database for rending airport layout, but extensible to any available standard database format. The graphical taxi route is provided using a protocol that has been developed specifically for this application, since there is no current standard available for this of information.
Update Rate	Approximately once per second. Depending on hardware, complexity of database and features to be drawn. display rendering is updated at between 15 and 60 Hz.

Airport Information Elements Depicted	
Runways	Grey
Runway centerlines	White
Runway labels	Black text in white text boxes
Taxiways	Grey
Taxiway centerlines	White
Taxiway labels	White characters in blue text boxes
Hold lines	Yellow
Non-movement areas	Grey
Ramp areas	Grey
Grassy areas	Green
Buildings	Black
Building labels	--
Other	Gates (black)

Functions Supported	
Ownship Depiction	Ownship is depicted as a white triangle at high map ranges (i.e., greater than 400 m) and a white aircraft icon at close map ranges. The symbol changes color due to alert conditions.
Indicators	
Conditions	Runway incursion alerting, hold violation, and route deviation alerting
Visual Indicators	Runway incursion alerting for traffic conflict: The runway is depicted in red when there is a conflict, and a text message is presented at the bottom of the display to provide the pilot with information about the conflict. Additionally, ownship color changes to red. Color and symbol optimization is currently in work. Hold violation alerting: When crossing the hold line between the cleared part of the taxi route and the non-cleared part of the taxi, the ownship symbol turns red and a text message is presented at the bottom of the display. Route deviation alerting: When the aircraft is deviating a certain distance from the route, the ownship symbol will turn red and a text message is presented at the bottom of the display.

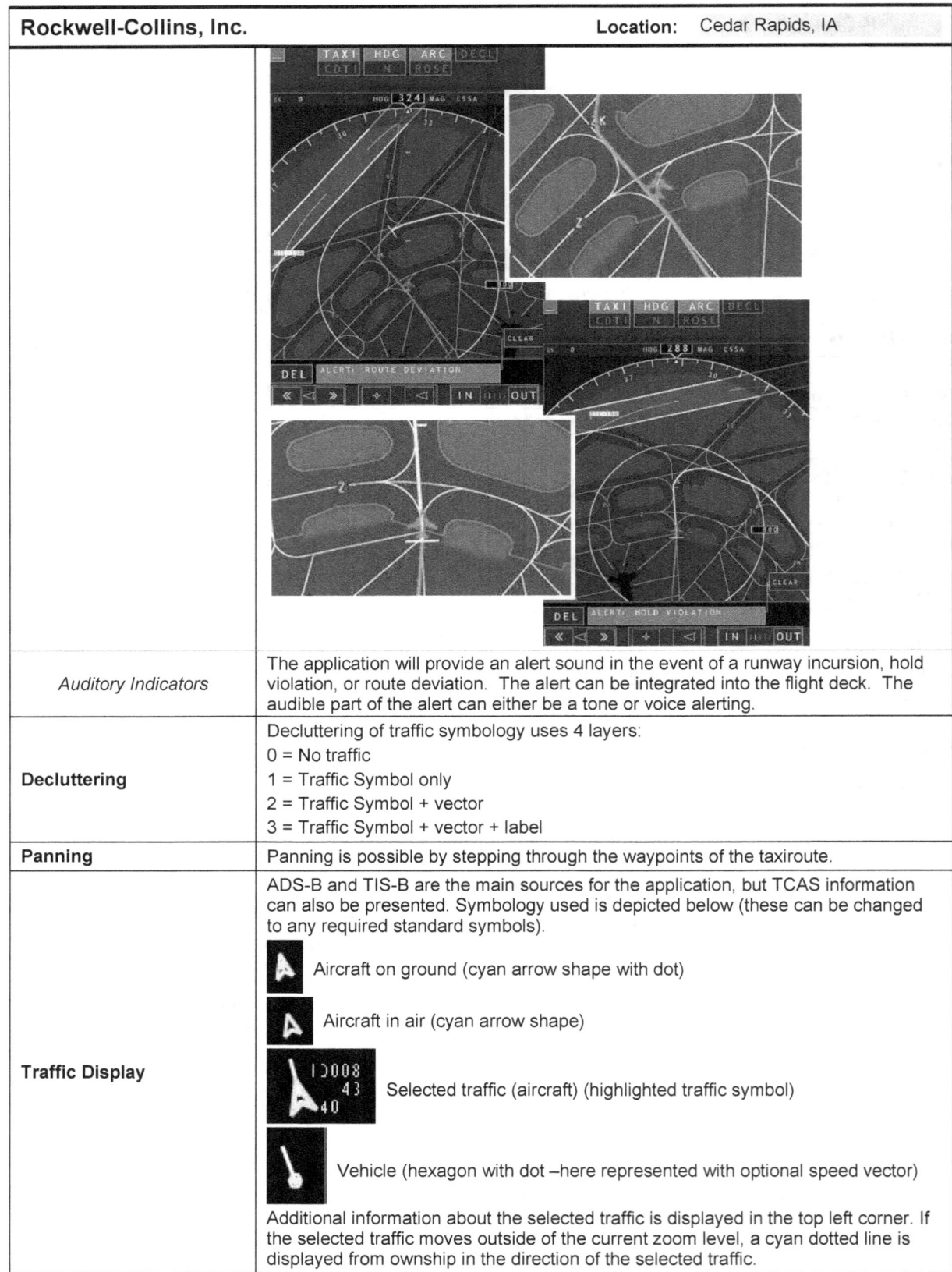

Auditory Indicators	The application will provide an alert sound in the event of a runway incursion, hold violation, or route deviation. The alert can be integrated into the flight deck. The audible part of the alert can either be a tone or voice alerting.
Decluttering	Decluttering of traffic symbology uses 4 layers: 0 = No traffic 1 = Traffic Symbol only 2 = Traffic Symbol + vector 3 = Traffic Symbol + vector + label
Panning	Panning is possible by stepping through the waypoints of the taxiroute.
Traffic Display	ADS-B and TIS-B are the main sources for the application, but TCAS information can also be presented. Symbology used is depicted below (these can be changed to any required standard symbols). Aircraft on ground (cyan arrow shape with dot) Aircraft in air (cyan arrow shape) Selected traffic (aircraft) (highlighted traffic symbol) Vehicle (hexagon with dot –here represented with optional speed vector) Additional information about the selected traffic is displayed in the top left corner. If the selected traffic moves outside of the current zoom level, a cyan dotted line is displayed from ownship in the direction of the selected traffic.

Route Guidance	The taxi route is graphically overlaid on top of the airport map. The taxi route is received by data link and also contains clearance information. The cleared part of the taxi route is visualized with a magenta line and the remaining part after the (virtual) hold is a yellow line. Any update to the route or clearance information has to be acknowledged/accepted by the pilot using the interface of the EFB. Taxi route information is completely independent of the airport database that is depicted. Taxi route information is generated by the controller at the airport. The generator of the taxi route should be aware of construction and/or other events that impact taxi instructions. NOTAMS are not depicted in this implementation.
Zooming/Autozoom	Range settings in ground mode have 5 levels from 400 ft to 6400 ft for the radius of the inner range circle (manually selectable). No autozoom.

TerraVision Ltd.		Location: Petah Tikva, Israel
Product(s)	*FollowTheGreen✈*	
Website(s)	www.terravision.co.il	
Approvals / Compliance	*Avionics Box Type :* ☐ Installed/MFD ☒ EFB (Class ☒ 1 ☒ 2 ☐ 3) *Authority:* ☒ FAA ☐ EASA ☒ Other (CAA) *Type of Approval/Compliance* TSO: ☐ C113 ☒ C165 ☐ C166A ☐ Other AC: ☐ AC 20-159 ☐ AC120-76A ☐ TC ☐ STC *Aircraft:* _____ ☐ Order 8900.1 ☒ RTCA DO-178B (Level _D_)	

Product Overview

FTG✈ is an AMMD (Aerodrome Moving Map Display) software application that incorporates all standard requirements per RTCA DO-257A with overlay data management capabilities. *FTG✈* is a database driven application compliant with RTCA DO-272A. *FTG✈* utilizes a graphics engine designed and developed specifically for the AMMD application by TerraVision. *FTG✈* is structured using flexible architecture and can be adapted to any EFB Class 1 and Class 2 hardware systems.

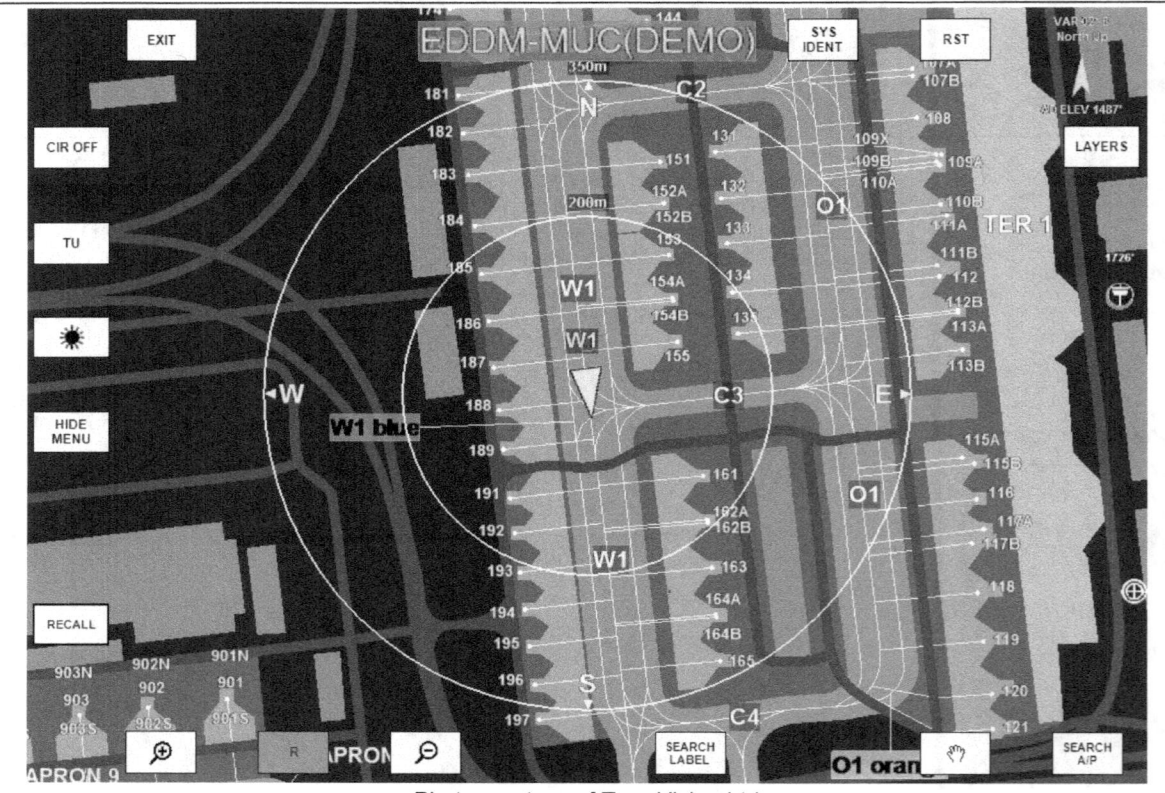

Photo courtesy of TerraVision Ltd.

Hardware Platform	EFB class 2 (Installed) and class 1 (Laptop)
Display Size	*FTG✈* can be adapted to any size of display and resolution

TerraVision Ltd.		**Location:** Petah Tikva, Israel
Data Format	☐ Raster ☐ Vector ☒ Database *Format* ☒ ARINC Specification 816 *Standards* ☒ RTCA DO-200A ☒ RTCA DO-272 *Other:* The structure of the database allows continuous updates and modifications. (TerraVision also provides AMDBs (Aerodrome Map Data Bases) with better than medium accuracy and routine integrity as specified in RTCA DO-272A.	
Update Rate	When connected to avionics data the frame rate is at least 10 Hz to meet data transfer rates. While panning the frame rate is 50 Hz.	

Airport Information Elements Depicted

Runways	Light Grey
Runway centerlines	White
Runway labels	White text in dark grey text boxes
Taxiways	Dark grey
Taxiway centerlines	Yellow
Taxiway labels	Yellow text in black text boxes
Hold lines	Tomato
Non-movement areas	Black
Apron areas	Dark grey
Grassy areas	Black
Buildings	Blue
Building labels	White
Other	Runway markings: white Closed RWY/Taxi: brown outline Service roads: dark grey Stand guidance line: yellow Parking stand location: white Runway exit line: white Runway shoulders: brown

Functions Supported

Ownship Depiction	Ownship is presented and depicted as a green triangle. At low speeds when heading information is unreliable, ownship is depicted as a green circle.
Indicators	Runway Incursion alert Selected parking stand
Conditions	Runway incursion indication thresholds are based on distance between ownship to Runway, the A/C speed and the geometric between the aircraft vector (Heading) and the runway. Parking stand indication is based on user selection.

TerraVision Ltd.	Location: Petah Tikva, Israel

Visual Indicators	A runway incursion is indicated by changing the map background color, and showing a text message in the designated messages area at the lower left corner of the display. The message text identifies the runway (e.g., "**Entering RWY 07L-25R**"); the color of the message is yellow. (See figure below) 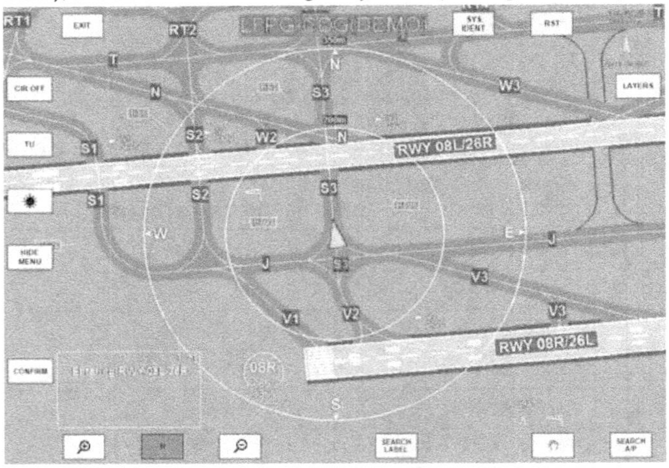 The selected parking stand is highlighted in orange and cyan. 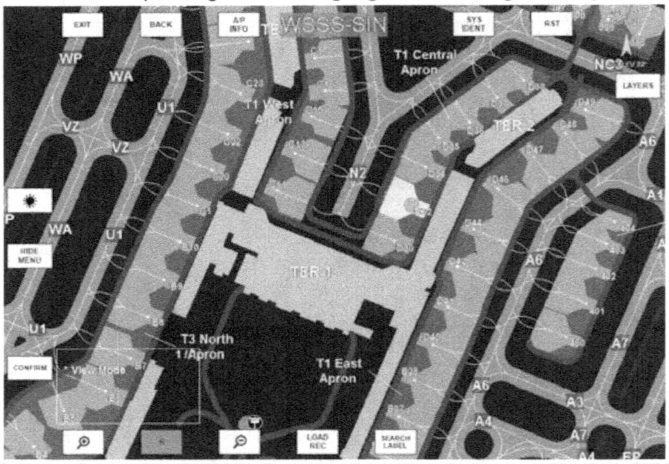
Auditory Indicators	No auditory information is available (at this stage)
Decluttering	Map layers (i.e., geometric elements such as taxi element, runway markings and such) are decluttered according to zoom level automatically for cartographic readability. Information layers are divided into sub-categories, each sub-category may further divided into sub-layers, each sub-layer display is user selectable.
Panning	Yes
Traffic Display	Under development. Traffic is not currently depicted, although the system's infrastructure is built to support it.
Route Guidance	Under development. Taxi information is not currently depicted, although the system's infrastructure is built to support it.
Zooming/Autozoom	Zoom in, Zoom out, and Zooming to initial Zoom and zoom to selected area are provided. There are 10 levels of zoom ranging from 50% to 500%.

THALES	Location: Toulouse, France

Product(s)	**Airport Navigation Product Line**
Website(s)	• www.thalesgroup.com • OANS (Onboard Airport Navigation System)
Approvals / Compliance	*Avionics Box Type :* ☒ Installed/MFD ☐ EFB (Class ☐ 1 ☐ 2 ☐ 3) *Authority:* ☒ FAA ☒ EASA ☐ Other *Type of Approval/Compliance* TSO: ☐ C113 ☐ C165 ☐ C166A ☐ Other AC: ☐ AC 20-159 ☐ AC120-76A ☒ TC ☐ STC *Aircraft:* A380 ☐ Order 8900.1 ☒ RTCA DO-178B (Level C)

Product Overview

For over a decade, Thales has been involved in defining future airport surface functions through several internal, national and European Research and Development programs. Some of the results of this research have been implemented in the **Airport Navigation Product Line,** which is intended to provide the flight crew with information to enhance situation awareness to support safety and efficiency during airport surface operations for all regional, business and air transport aircraft. Ownship position is displayed dynamically on the aircraft's Navigation Displays, using a high-resolution geo-referenced airport moving map, by using an Airport Mapping Database (AMDB). During flight operations, pilots can access information through a cursor control device to consult the airport map and to prepare routing on the selected airport. On the ground, pilots are presented with information to support taxiing operations from and to the gate, including alerting functions, such as Approaching Runway and Runway Overrun, to help the flight crew avoid potential runway incursions or excursions. Other functions under development for the Airport Navigation Systems solution are intended to support upcoming airport surface operations enhancements through information sharing with ATC and other avionics components (such as traffic display and taxi route uplinks). These functions introduce the potential for additional advisories and alerts, e.g., surface traffic conflict detection and alerting, potential route deviations, exit guidance.

The OANS version is already available and used on Airbus A380, and will be progressively deployed on A320/A330/A340 families then A350. Development of other versions on other aircraft types is also under way.

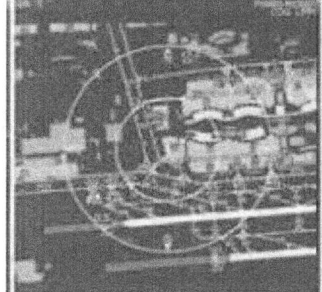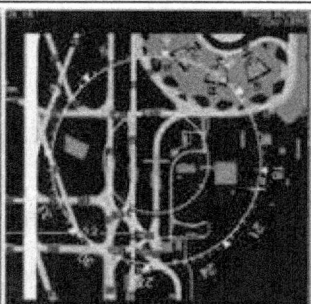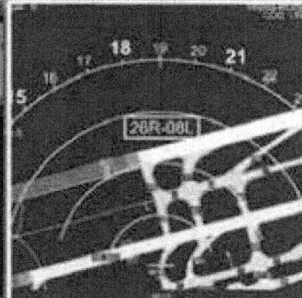

Photo Credit: Jack Burlot, Airbus Industrie.

Hardware Platform	The Surface Moving Map application is presented on existing aircraft Navigation Displays (ND). It can be displayed simultaneously on each of the two NDs, with each showing a potentially different airport, range or display mode (ARC, ROSE, or PLAN). Airport Navigation application is either installed on a dedicated stand-alone LRU or integrated into an avionics suite or in the Navigation Displays. Airport Navigation Research and Development programs have examined the use of Class 2 EFBs, which may be appropriate for some basic functions. However, advanced functions would need to be presented on installed avionics since several other systems would be needed for achieving the function (e.g. Flight Warning Computer, FMS, Braking Units, Communication Units, etc). The use of a Head-Up Display (HUD) is also being considered.

THALES	Location: Toulouse, France
Display Size	Varies depending on the ND on which the application is hosted
Data Format	☐ Raster ☐ Vector ☒ Database *Format* ☐ ARINC Specification 816 *Standards* ☐ RTCA DO-200A ☒ RTCA DO-272 *Other:* RTCA DO-160D, RTCA DO-254 Level C
Update Rate	Function of the aircraft installation: typically in the 10 - 15 Hz range

Airport Information Elements Depicted

The details may vary from one installation to another or from one research prototype to another. The description provided in this section corresponds to the depiction shown in the images above.

Runways	White
Runway centerlines	Yes
Runway labels	White
Taxiways	Grey
Taxiway centerlines	Yes
Taxiway labels	Yellow text in black box
Hold lines	Yes
Non-movement areas	Black
Ramp areas	Grey
Grassy areas	Black
Buildings	Blue
Building labels	Blue in black box
Other	

Functions Supported

Ownship Depiction	Ownship is presented using an aircraft symbol. Color depends on aircraft installation. (typically purple or yellow)
Indicators	Several alert types (shown on ND, with potential specific message displayed on PFD and potential aural messages)
Visual Indicators	Varies depending on aircraft installations. Note that some of the functions listed below are still under study. Runway Alerting • Selected Runway advisory: the runway outline is highlighted on the SMM. The color of the highlighting varies depending on the installation. Highlighting is performed permanently as soon as the selected runway is designated by the crew. No text message is shown. • Approaching Runway alert (on-ground) : the runway outline is highlighted and flashing on the SMM with a text label superimposed on the SMM (typically "Approaching Runway" or display of Runway extremity labels) as soon as the aircraft is approaching a runway from a taxiway • Approaching Runway advisory (in-flight): the runway outline is highlighted on the SMM with no text label superimposed on the SMM as soon as the aircraft is approaching a runway. • Approaching occupied runway, with or without clearance (on-ground and in-flight)

THALES	Location: Toulouse, France
	Braking Guidance • Braking cues: dedicated lines are overlaid on the runway on the SMM • Runway Overrun : a dedicated symbol is overlaid on the SMM, with a specific message displayed on the PFDs. Implementation may also include a potential aural alert Other Alerts and Indications • Surface traffic conflict detection and alerting • Taxi Alerting, e.g., wrong direction, weight not compatible, etc. • Steering guidance indications • Exit Guidance indications
Auditory Indicators	
Decluttering	Decluttering is function of display range.
Panning	Yes (with the use of the Control Cursor Device)
Traffic Display	In development: traffic will be received from the Traffic Computer (e.g., TCAS, ADS-B).
Route Guidance	Varies depending on aircraft installations. Taxi route could be manually entered through an interactive means, a predefined route could be selected from taxi route database, or the route could be uplinked from ATC (e.g., through CPDLC). The color used to depict the route also varies depending on the installation.
Zooming/Autozoom	Different selectable ranges. No Autozoom.
Other Functions	• Airport Database Uplinks for updates or NOTAMS • Taxi assistance with line deviation indication • Automated guidance

4   RESEARCH DISPLAYS

BAE Systems, Technische Universität Darmstadt (AMM Developer), University of Malta, Deep Blue

Location:

Product(s)	Airborne Integrated Systems for Safety Improvement, Flight Hazard Protection and All Weather Operations (FLYSAFE)
Website(s)	www.eu-flysafe.org
Approvals	Research display - No approvals from certification authorities

Product Overview

FLYSAFE is an integrated project, sponsored by the European Commission, to research and design a Next Generation Integrated Surveillance System (NG ISS). As part of this effort, FLYSAFE is developing systems and functions intended to improve situation awareness and provide advanced warning for potential threats (e.g., traffic collision, ground collision, and weather). One of the systems is a surface moving map, which is intended to provide enhanced traffic situational awareness on the airport surface (ATSA-SURF). Taxi route, runway clearances, and traffic alerting functions are included.

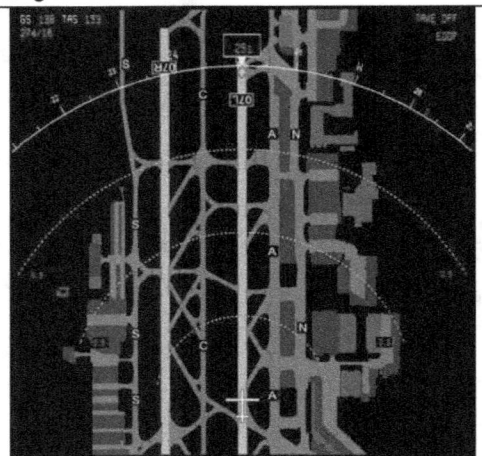 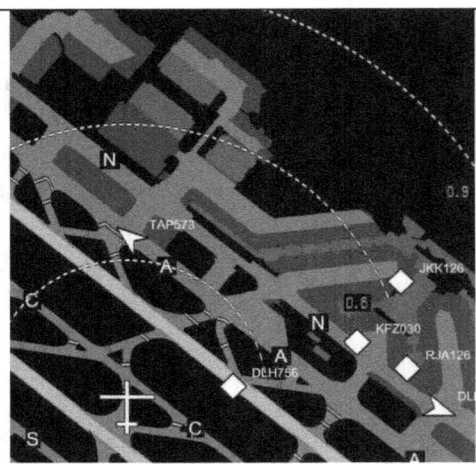

Photo courtesy of FLYSAFE research consortium.

Hardware Platform	Navigation Display
Display Size	Intended for a standard glass-cockpit Navigation Display
Data Format	Database-driven – ED-99 / ED-99A
Update Rate	Varying with the number of objects / complexity of textures and hardware. Currently at least 20 fps are achieved.

Airport Information Elements Depicted

Runways	Light grey Closed runways indicated with red x's along the runway Active runway: white x's superimposed over the runway indicate closure for takeoff and landings The FMS Runway is highlighted with a white boarder.
Runway centerlines	White
Runway labels	White text in black text box The label is "dimmed" (white text in grey text box) to indicate non-active runway
Taxiways	Dark grey
Taxiway centerlines	Yellow
Taxiway labels	Yellow text in black text box
Hold lines	Red

	BAE Systems, Technische Universität Darmstadt (AMM Developer), University of Malta, Deep Blue	Location:
Non-movement areas	Black	
Ramp areas	Dark grey	
Grassy areas	Black	
Buildings	Blue	
Building labels	--	
Other		
Functions Supported		
Ownship Depiction	Yellow aircraft icon	

	Threat	Alerting means	Aural Message	Text message	Visual Indicator	Alert Level (DI 1.2.5) [1]
Indicators	Runway incursion	3D PFD, ND, aural alert	RUNWAY INCURSION	PFD: "RWY INCURSION" ND: "RUNWAY INCURSION"	Yes	3
	(Intruder either on final approach or taking off)	3D PFD, ND, aural alert	TRAFFIC ON APPROACH	PFD: "APPROACHING TRAFFIC" ND: "APPROACHING TRAFFIC"	Yes	2
	Ground traffic on taxiway	3D PFD, ND, Aural alert	GROUND TRAFFIC	PFD: "GROUND TRAFFIC" ND: "GROUND TRAFFIC"	Yes	2
		3D PFD, ND	GROUND TRAFFIC	PFD: "GROUND TRAFFIC" ND: "GROUND TRAFFIC"	Yes	1
	Runway incursion	ND, aural alert	RUNWAY INCURSION	PFD: "RWY INCURSION" ND: "RUNWAY INCURSION"	Yes	3
		ND, aural alert	RUNWAY INCURSION	PFD: "RWY INCURSION" ND:"RUNWAY NCURSION"	Yes	3
		3D PFD, ND, aural alert	TRAFFIC ON APPROACH	PFD: "APPROACHING TRAFFIC" ND: "APPROACHING TRAFFIC"	Yes	2
		3D PFD, ND, aural alert	TRAFFIC ON APPROACH	PFD: "APPROACH NG TRAFFIC" ND: "APPROACHING TRAFFIC"	Yes	2
Conditions	Traffic alerts are based on spatial proximity between aircraft and closure rates. Alerting thresholds are currently subject of further refinement for the main task evaluation.					

BAE Systems, Technische Universität Darmstadt (AMM Developer), University of Malta, Deep Blue	Location:

Visual Indicators	Traffic Alerts: conflict traffic is drawn in amber Runway incursion alerts: runway is highlighted in red for a warning, conflict aircraft on the runway (and data tag) is also drawn in red Traffic Alert Runway Incursion Alert
Auditory Indicators	See "Indicators"
Decluttering	Manual decluttering is provided: Airport – everything except runways on/off Traffic – Labels on/off Automatic Traffic decluttering: All traffic on the airport disappears if the selected range does not enable to distinguish the different traffic elements.
Panning	--
Traffic Display	Yes, white chevrons Part of the FLYSAFE NG-ISS is the Traffic Data Fusion System which access ADS-B, TIS-B, TCAS and other sources to provide traffic information to other subsystems. More detail on its structure is provided in "The European Research Project FLYSAFE: Evaluation of Novel Traffic Functionalities for Future Airliners", presented at the Council of the European Aerospace Societies (CEAS) 2007 by N. Barraci; C. Vernaleken; C. Urvoy; K. Koch; A. Andreas, Sindlinger, DE; G. Heidelmeyer; and U. Klingauf.
Route Guidance	Yes, green line
Zooming/Autozoom	Zooming is provided, no auto-zoom.

Delft University of Technology		Location: Delft, The Netherlands
Product(s)	Safe Airport Navigation	
Website(s)	• http://www.synthetic-vision.tudelft.nl/SVatDelftUofT/SVatDelftUofT.htm • www.stw.nl/Projecten/D/det/det5844.htm	
Approvals	N/A. Research only.	

Product Overview

Delft University of Technology developed a surface guidance system for research purposes through the "Safe Airport Navigation" project, sponsored by the Dutch Technology Foundation. The goal of the program is to examine whether it is possible to compensate for reduced visibility conditions through the presentation of navigation and communication on a surface map display, e.g., by providing route information and taxi instructions. The Surface Movement Guidance system consists of two components: a plan view navigation display to support global awareness of ownship position on the airport surface, and a taxi guidance display to support local awareness for route-following.

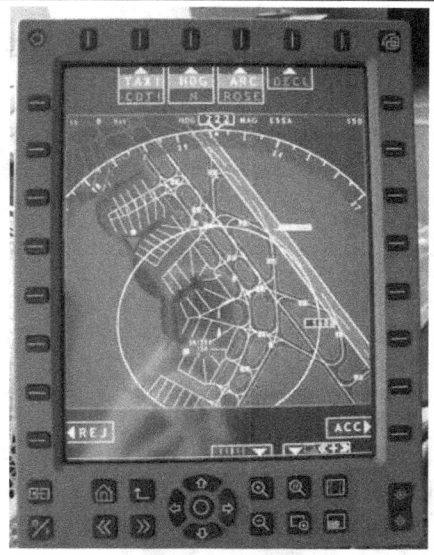 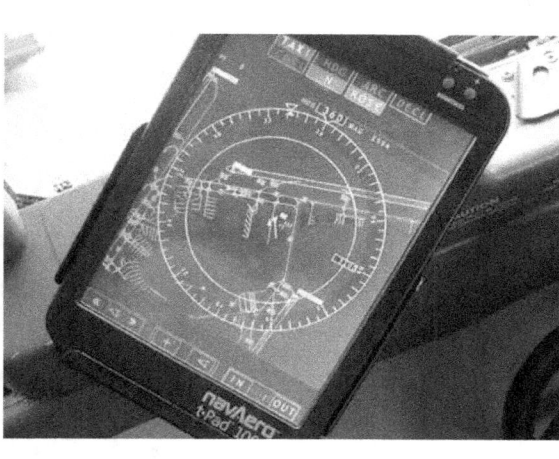

The figure on the left shows an implementation in the plan-view mode on a BFGoodrich EFB. The figure on the right shows the implementation adapted for a touchscreen display using a NavAero EFB.

Photos courtesy of E. Theunissen, Delft University of Technology.

Hardware Platform	Class 3 EFB (simulation). Platforms used: Panasonic Toughbook, BFGoodrich EFB, NavAero EFB.
Display Size	768 x 1024 pixels (125 x 170 mm)
Data Format	Database-driven, internal proprietary format. The primary source for the database is information from airport surveys conducted by the FAA Safe Flight 21 program.
Update Rate	> 10 Hz

Airport Information Elements Depicted

Runways	Grey
Runway centerlines	--
Runway labels	Black text in white text boxes
Taxiways	Grey
Taxiway centerlines	Grey
Taxiway labels	White characters in blue text boxes

Delft University of Technology	Location: Delft, The Netherlands
Hold lines	Yellow
Non-movement areas	Grey
Ramp areas	Grey
Grassy areas	Green
Buildings	Black
Building labels	--
Other	
Functions Supported	
Ownship Depiction	Yes. White triangle . Icon changes to a white aircraft icon when closely zoomed in (forward range set to 400 m).
Indicators	Route deviations Hold short violations Runway incursions
Conditions	The evaluations so far used a static threshold for route deviation alerting. In case cross track error is greater than 15 meters, a route deviation is declared. In case the computed forward point of the aircraft has crossed an active hold position, a hold violation is declared. The most recent version of the EFB uses predictive alerting. The algorithm uses a combination of cross track error, track angle error and velocity to determine whether a future violation of the position constraint is likely, resulting in a dynamic threshold for the cross track error.
Visual Indicators	Route deviation or hold-short violation: ownship is colored red Runway incursion: Runway is colored red and the conflict aircraft shown in yellow. Route deviation

Delft University of Technology	**Location:** Delft, The Netherlands

Hold short violation
Photos courtesy of E. Theunissen, Delft University of Technology.

Auditory Indicators	Only an attenson ping to attract the pilot's attention for route deviations, hold short violation, or potential runway incursion. There is no specific verbal warning or alerting.
Decluttering	3-level declutter scheme for traffic symbols and taxiway labels (symbol only, symbol + vector, symbol + vector + labels).
Panning	No free panning. User can step through taxi route waypoints while display will center around active waypoint.
Traffic Display	TCAS traffic: non-directional symbol (diamond) ADS-B traffic : white unfilled chevron; velocity vector can be added
Route Guidance	Yes. The route is depicted graphically and listed textually at the bottom of the display. Cleared route information is drawn in magenta and pending is drawn in yellow. The textual route information lists ownship's current taxiway/runway and the next four taxiways/runways. *Photos courtesy of E. Theunissen, Delft University of Technology.*
Zooming/Autozoom	Five zoom levels (400 m, 800 m, 1600 m, 3200 m, 6400 m range from ownship) no autozoom.

MITRE		Location: McLean, Virginia
Product(s)	MITRE CAASD Cockpit Display of Traffic Information (CDTI) prototype	
Website(s)	www.mitre.org	
Approvals	N/A. Research only. The research is intended to support requirements development of RTCA special committee 186, Working Group 1 for cockpit based runway safety indications and alerting.	

Product Overview

MITRE is conducting research concerning indications for normal and non-normal conditions on the airport surface. The capabilities assume the use of surveillance capabilities on board the aircraft such as ADS-B. The research prototypes depicted are intended to allow human-in-the-loop concept validations to support the development of national and international standards.

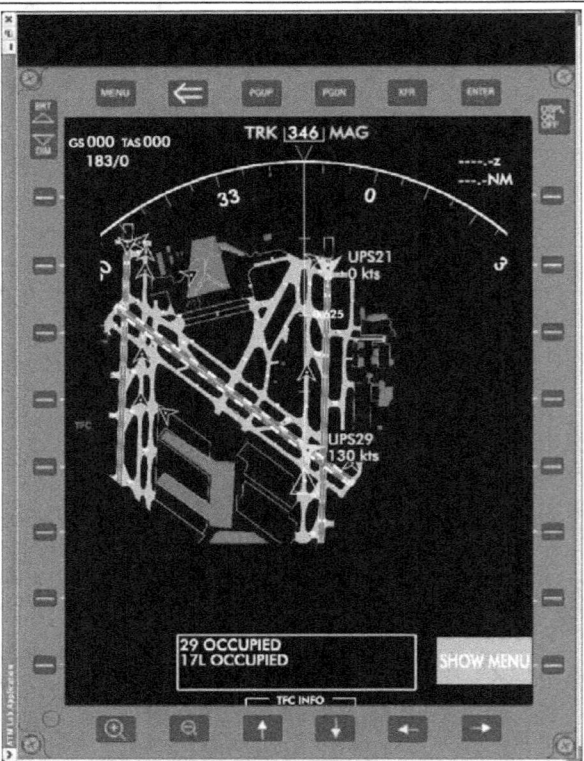

Photo courtesy of MITRE.

Hardware Platform	Research display. Class 2 or 3 EFB
Display Size	Diagonal display is 11 inches, resolution is 1024 x 768.
Data Format	Database-driven display
Update Rate	The display has a one second update rate.

Airport Information Elements Depicted

Runways	Dark Grey
Runway centerlines	White
Runway labels	White
Taxiways	Light grey
Taxiway centerlines	--

MITRE	Location: McLean, Virginia
Taxiway labels	White characters in black text box
Hold lines	--
Non-movement areas	Black
Ramp areas	Black
Grassy areas	Black
Buildings	Blue
Building labels	--
Other	

Functions Supported	
Ownship Depiction	Yes. White unfilled triangle
Indicators	Traffic display with ownship position and runway safety indicators and alerts
Conditions	Runway Safety Indications identify runway and traffic status as relevant to own-ship operations. Traffic, as viewed from ownship's current state is considered "relevant" if that traffic position, orientation, and movement could potentially lead to a runway incursion or collision within a foreseeable period of time. Indications are intended to identify normal operational conditions to the flight crew that are generally relevant for runway safety and could be a precursor to a runway safety hazard. Indications are not intended to attract pilot awareness. Primary indications are provided if ownship's runway is not usable for taxi, takeoff or landing by ownship. Secondary indications are provided if the runway is currently usable by ownship but there could be a potential collision hazard in the immediate future. Indications are generally provided as a function of ownship position in relation to the runway. In contrast to indications, runway safety alerts are intended to help prevent potential collisions between two aircraft. Alerts are intended to attract pilot awareness. Alerts are provided as a function of position and closure rate between ownship and conflict traffic. Caution alerts are intended to provide immediate flight crew awareness for subsequent flight crew response. Warnings are intended to facilitate immediate flight crew awareness for immediate response. Specific alerting behavior depends on the scenarios and both levels of alerts may not be triggered in all situations.
Visual Indicators	Blue-white outlined runway: indicates occupied runway with traffic that is relevant to ownship; the traffic aircraft is converging onto a common intersection Enlarged, filled-in chevron: indicates relevant traffic currently on a runway Flight identifier and ground speed: provides additional information about relevant traffic on a runway. Runway status box: provides textual information regarding runway occupancy, e.g., "[Runway number] occupied"

MITRE		Location: McLean, Virginia
	For Cautions: Occupied runway and conflict traffic aircraft are drawn in yellow; yellow text in the runway status box provides alert message ("CAUTION TRAFFIC ON [Runway number]") For Alerts: Occupied runway and conflict traffic aircraft are drawn in red; red text in the runway status box provides alert message ("WARNING TRAFFIC ON [Runway number]")	
Auditory Indicators	Indications: For situations when ownship is taxiing toward a runway entrance and traffic is approaching that intersection at high speed, an auditory message is presented such as: "Traffic Ahead" Caution and warning alerts are presented with an auditory message, for example: "Traffic Ahead"	
Decluttering	Does not allow decluttering.	
Panning	Does not allow panning.	
Traffic Display	ADS-B ground and airborne traffic is depicted on the display. Ground traffic is indicated as brown chevron with a dot in the center. Airborne traffic is depicted as blue chevron and altitude difference to ownship. 	
Route Guidance	The research prototype does not provide route guidance.	
Zooming/Autozoom	The research prototype only provides manual zooming. No automated zooming is provided.	

NASA-Ames Research Center	Location: Moffett Field, CA

Product(s)	Taxiway Navigation and Situation Awareness (T-NASA) System
Website(s)	• NASA-Ames Human Factors: humansystems.arc.nasa.gov • T-NASA: hsi.arc.nasa.gov/groups/HCSL/research/tnasa.html • Research reports: hsi.arc.nasa.gov/groups/HCSL/publications.html
Approvals	N/A

Product Overview

The Taxiway Navigation and Situation Awareness (T-NASA) System is a suite of research displays to aid pilot navigation on the airport surface. One of the components is a surface moving map that presents routing, guidance, and surveillance information. The map is considered to be a secondary display, since it is integrated with a head-up display that is intended to be the primary source for navigation. NASA-Ames is no longer actively working on T NASA, although research to improve the efficiency and safety of taxi operations continues using variants of the display suite.

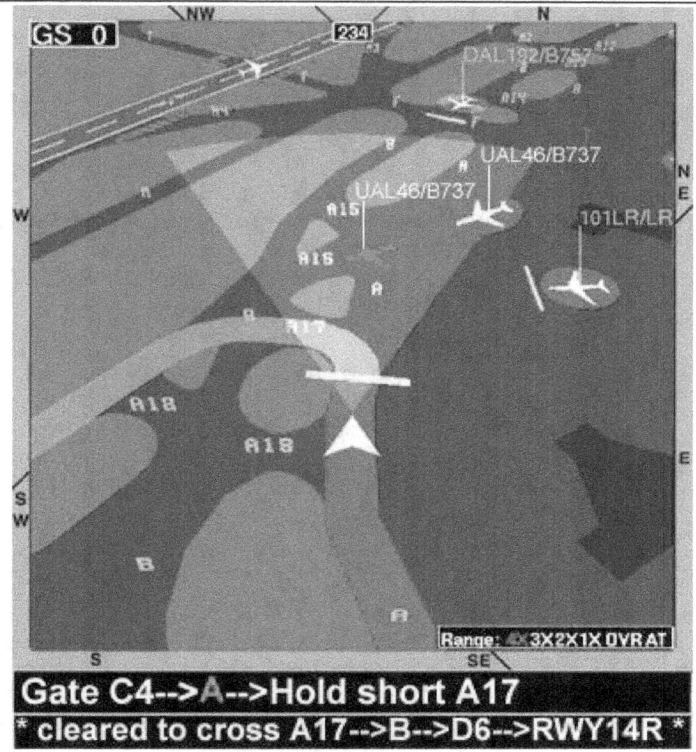

Photo courtesy of NASA-Ames.

Hardware Platform	Installed: the surface moving map application is located on the multifunction display used to show navigation information.
Display Size	6 x 6 in (Navigation Display)
Data Format	Database-driven
Update Rate	60Hz

Airport Information Elements Depicted

Some aspects of the design of this research display, in its current form, may preclude certification, based on guidance in regulatory documents. For example, the color red is used inappropriately to highlight the current zoom level. Regulatory documents (e.g., 14 CFR §§ 23.1322, 25.1322, 27.1322, 29.1322 and RTCA DO-257A) limit the use of red for indicating a hazard that may require immediate corrective action.

Runways	Black. Red lines across intersections indicate occupancy.
Runway centerlines	--
Runway labels	White

NASA-Ames Research Center	Location: Moffett Field, CA
Taxiways	Black
Taxiway centerlines	--
Taxiway labels	White
Hold lines	Red bar surrounded by yellow border
Non-movement areas	Black
Ramp areas	Black
Grassy areas	Green
Buildings	Blue
Building labels	--
Other	--
Functions Supported	
Ownship Depiction	White triangular symbol indicating position and directionality
Indicators	• Runway occupancy • Traffic incursion • ATC Hold bars for ownship and other aircraft • Cardinal ordinate positions are shown on edge (e.g., E = East; SW = Southwest) and move as appropriate • Forward "visual cone" reference to highlight approximate forward view and forward distance indication (800m Distance)
Conditions	Hold bars based on ATC clearances
Visual Indicators	• Runway occupancy: Indicated with red bars outlining the runway, simulating AMASS-like technology. • Traffic incursions: three stage color-coding scheme (white, yellow, red), similar to TCAS. • Ownship taxi clearance provided in text via datalink at bottom of display
Auditory Indicators	• Traffic incursions: Direction tone + "Traffic – Traffic" • Hold Short crossing: Non-directional tone + "Hold Short" issued when ownship crosses an active hold bar (i.e., violates an ATC hold clearance) • Route deviations: Non-directional tone + "Off Route" when ownship deviates from the cleared taxi route
Decluttering	Yes. Can show all traffic or only traffic within a specified radius from the ownship.
Panning	No
Traffic Display	White aircraft icon, when accurate directional information is available. Otherwise, a solid circle is used with optional ID (aircraft type and call sign) To indicate the likelihood of an incursion with other traffic, the color of the conflict aircraft changes from white to yellow and then to red.
Route Guidance	Taxi route is depicted as a thick magenta strip for cleared routes. Hold short directives are incorporated by depicting yellow flashing hold bars for ownship and traffic. The cleared route, pending the hold, is shown in yellow and pending routes are shown in flashing white. A text display of the taxi route is provided below the display.
Zooming/Autozoom	Zooming provided over four levels (all perspective views), plus one overview (plan view). No autozoom capability.

NASA-Langley		**Location:** Hampton, VA

Product(s)	Runway Incursion Prevention System (RIPS)
Website(s)	• NASA-Langley: www.nasa.gov/centers/langley/home/index.html • www.nasa.gov/centers/langley/news/factsheets/RIPS.html • Work conducted under a cooperative agreement with ERA (see www.erabeyondradar.com)
Approvals	N/A

Product Overview

NASA-Langley's RIPS effort was built on NASA-Ames' Taxiway Navigation and Situation Awareness (T-NASA) System. In RIPS, incursion alerts are presented visually on the surface map and are accompanied by an auditory warning. These alerts are generated by the Runway Safety Monitor (RSM) conflict detection algorithm developed for NASA by Lockheed Martin. A second runway conflict detection algorithm, PathProx™, has also been developed by ERA Corporation, under a cooperative agreement with NASA-Langley.

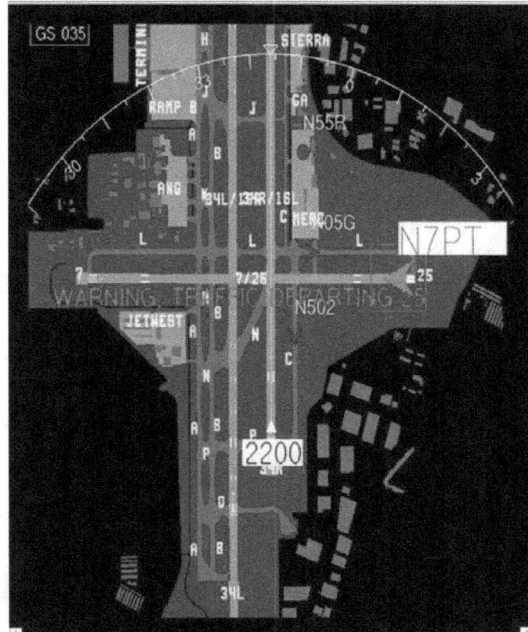 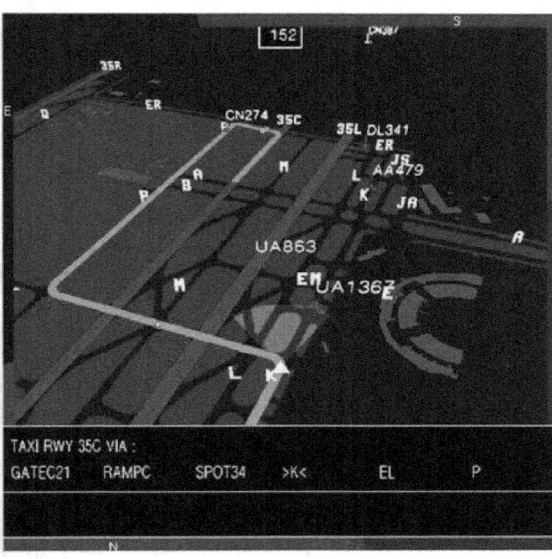

Photo courtesy of NASA-Langley.

Hardware Platform	Simulation. Class 3 EFB, Navigation Display
Display Size	10." Diagonal, 1280 x 1024 pixel resolution
Data Format	Database-driven
Update Rate	Adjustable

Airport Information Elements Depicted
Information provided reflects implementation on a plan-view display

Runways	Grey
Runway centerlines	White
Runway labels	Yellow
Taxiways	Brown
Taxiway centerlines	--
Taxiway labels	Yellow

NASA-Langley	Location: Hampton, VA
Hold lines	--
Non-movement areas	Black
Ramp areas	Black
Grassy areas	Green
Buildings	Brown
Building labels	--
Other	--
Functions Supported	
Ownship Depiction	Yes. White triangle. Solid when on ground, open when airborne.
Indicators	Runway incursion / conflict alerts, hold short violation alerts, deviation from assigned taxi route alerts
Conditions	RSM uses a generic approach for detecting and generating incursion alerts and monitors traffic that enters a three-dimensional virtual protection zone around the runway that is being used by the ownship. Incursion detection is based on the operational state of the ownship and traffic, as well as other criteria (separation and closure rate). Identification, position, and altitude data is used to track the traffic in the protection zone. PathProx™ uses a scenario based algorithm for detecting conflicts. The algorithm incorporates scenarios that capture all potential runway incursion conflicts. Cautions and warnings are generated based on aircraft states and separation (distance and time).
Visual Indicators	Alert phrases provide information regarding location of incurring traffic, e.g., "Warning Traffic Departing 25", "Caution, Traffic 34 R. Text information is presented in yellow for cautions and red for warnings. The traffic symbol for the incurring aircraft is highlighted by a designator box and drawn at a larger size and different color (yellow for cautions and red for warnings). If the incurring traffic is not on the display, a symbol at the edge of the display in the direction of the traffic aircraft's location is shown.
Auditory Indicators	Auditory alerts present audible annunciation of the visual text conflict alerts. Audible alerts are also given for hold short violations and deviation from assigned taxi route.
Decluttering	Yes. ATC messages, traffic information tag
Panning	No
Traffic Display	Yes Ground traffic displayed as dark blue chevrons; airborne traffic displayed as cyan chevrons. Traffic sources include simulated traffic, ADS-B, TIS-B.
Route Guidance	The taxi route is shown in magenta and provided in text form in a pop-up window. Hold short locations are depicted as a red bar outlined in yellow.
Zooming/Autozoom	Multiple zoom levels (0.5 nm, 1 nm, 1.5 nm, 2 nm, 2.5 nm, 5 nm, 10 nm, 20 nm, 40 nm, 60 nm, 80 nm, 160 nm) No autozoom.

Technische Universität Darmstadt	Location: Darmstadt, Germany
Product(s)	Airport Moving Map
Website(s)	www.fsr.tu-darmstadt.de/research/groups/en_cavok.html
Approvals	Research display - No approvals from certification authorities

Product Overview

The Airport Moving Map developed in TUDs Research Flight Deck Displays aims at improving the flight crew's situational awareness. The first step is the display of ownship on the airport moving map to help gain positional awareness. Awareness of surrounding traffic is enabled by the display of traffic data on this same map. Operational and Clearance awareness are obtained by displaying on the map information coming from the Preflight Information Bulletin (Runway Closures, Taxiway Closures, etc.) and clearance information in case CPDLC is available.

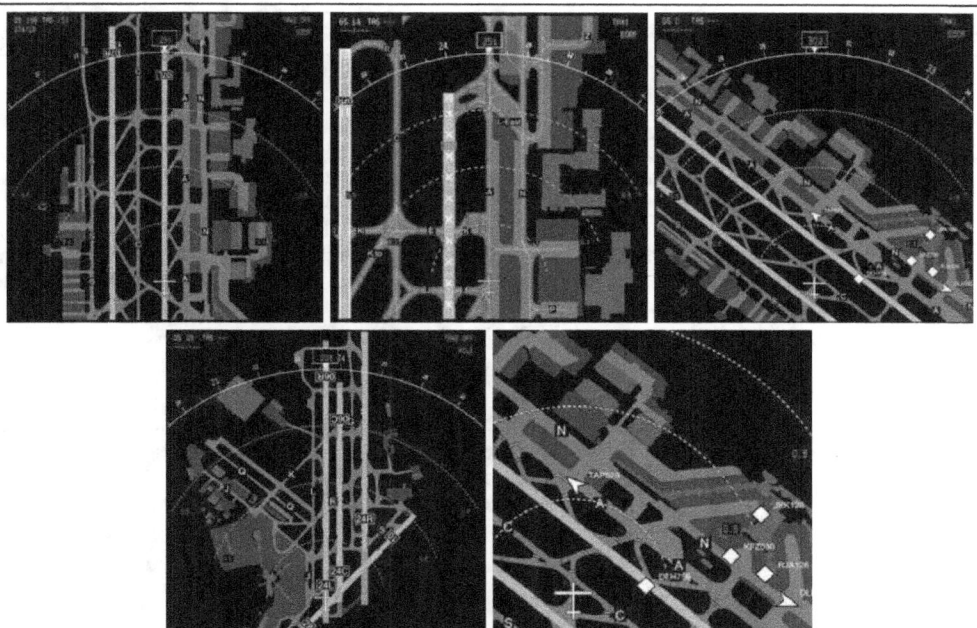

Photos provided courtesy of Technische Universität Darmstadt.

Hardware Platform	Navigation Display
Display Size	Intended for a standard glass-cockpit Navigation Display
Data Format	Database-driven – ED-99 / ED-99A
Update Rate	Varying with the number of objects / complexity of textures and hardware. Currently at least 20 fps are achieved.

Airport Information Elements Depicted

Runways	Light grey Closed runways indicated with red x's along the runway Active runway: white x's superimposed over the runway indicate closure for takeoff and landings The FMS Runway is highlighted with a white boarder.
Runway centerlines	White
Runway labels	White text in black text box The label is "dimmed" (white text in grey text box) to indicate non-active runway
Taxiways	Dark grey

Technische Universität Darmstadt	Location: Darmstadt, Germany
Taxiway centerlines	Yellow
Taxiway labels	Yellow text in black text box
Hold lines	Yellow. If information regarding ATC clearances is available, then the hold line corresponding to the end of ownship's clearance is highlighted in red.
Non-movement areas	Black
Ramp areas	Dark grey
Grassy areas	Black
Buildings	Blue
Building labels	--
Other	
Functions Supported	
Ownship Depiction	Yellow aircraft icon
Indicators	Indications were developed through a joint research effort with the FLYSAFE research consortium (see also the entry for BAE Systems, Technische Universität Darmstadt, University of Malta, and Deep Blue in this review). The concepts below are described in C. Vernalaken, C. Urvoy, and U. Klingauf, Runway incursion prevention by enhanced onboard surveillance: Concept for a surface movement awareness and alerting system. Presented at *Enhanced Solutions for Aircraft and Vehicle Surveillance (ESAVS 2007)*, March 2007, Bonn. • Preventative surface moving indications, e.g., - Entering runway - Takeoff or landing on a runway that is not part of the FMS flight plan - Takeoff on a runway that is shorter than the minimum runway length required for the aircraft or takeoff on a taxiway - Approach to a closed runway - Unauthorized runway entry, e.g., takeoff without clearance • Traffic alerts • Runway incursion indications, e.g., traffic on runway
Conditions	Preventative surface movement indications are based on extrapolated aircraft nosewheel position with respect to the runway protection zone. The runway protection zone consists of the runway and the part of the taxiway extending beyond the runway hold short position. Runway incursion indications are based on spatial proximity between the traffic aircraft and the runway protection zone. Traffic alerts are based on the spatial proximity between the traffic aircraft and ownship.
Visual Indicators	Runway incursion warning: runway is highlighted in red, conflict aircraft on the runway (and data tag) is drawn in red.
Auditory Indicators	
Decluttering	Manual decluttering is provided: • Airport – everything except runways on/off • Automatic Traffic decluttering: All traffic on the airport disappears if the selected range does not enable to distinguish the different traffic elements.
Panning	No

Technische Universität Darmstadt	Location: Darmstadt, Germany
Traffic Display	Yes, white chevrons
Route Guidance	Yes, green line
Zooming/Autozoom	Zooming is provided, no auto-zoom.

5   REFERENCES

1. ARINC Specification 816, *Embedded interchange Format for Airport Mapping Database*, December 2007.

2. Federal Aviation Administration, Advisory Circular (AC) 20-159, *Obtaining Design and Production Approval of Airport Moving Map Display Applications Intended for Electronic Flight Bag Systems*. April 30, 2007.

3. Federal Aviation Administration, Advisory Circular (AC) 25-11A, *Electronic Flight Deck Displays*. June 21, 2007.

4. Federal Aviation Administration, Advisory Circular (AC) 120-76A,. *Guidelines for the certification, airworthiness, and operational approval of electronic flight bag computing devices*, March 17, 2003.

5. Federal Aviation Administration, Order 8900.1, *Flight Standards Information Management System*, Electronic Flight Bag Operational Authorization Process (Volume 4, Chapter 15), February 5, 2009.

6. Federal Aviation Administration, Technical Standard Order (TSO)- C113, *Airborne Multipurpose Electronic Displays*, October 27, 1986.

7. Federal Aviation Administration, Technical Standard Order (TSO)-C165, *Electronic Map Display Equipment for Graphical Depiction of Aircraft Position*, September 30, 2003.

8. Federal Aviation Administration, Technical Standard Order (TSO)- C166A, *Extended Squitter Automatic Dependent Surveillance - Broadcast (ADS-B) and Traffic Information Service - Broadcast (TIS-B) Equipment Operating on the Radio Frequency of 1090 Megahertz (MHz)*, December 21, 2006

9. RTCA DO-257A, *Minimum Operational Performance Standards for the Depiction of Navigational Information on Electronic Maps*. June 25, 2003.

10. RTCA DO-178B, *Software Considerations in Airborne Systems and Equipment Certification*. December 1, 1992.

11. RTCA DO-200A, Standards for Processing Aeronautical Data. September 28, 1998.

12. RTCA DO-272/ED-99, *User Requirements for Aerodrome Mapping Information*.

13. Title 14 of the Code of Federal Regulations (CFR) 23.1322, Warning, caution, and advisory lights.

14. Title 14 of the Code of Federal Regulations (CFR) 25.1322, *Warning, caution, and advisory lights*.

15. Title 14 of the Code of Federal Regulations (CFR) 27.1322, *Warning, caution, and advisory lights*.

16. Title 14 of the Code of Federal Regulations (CFR) 29.1322, *Warning, caution, and advisory lights*.

17. Yeh, M. (2004). Human Factors Considerations in the Design and Evaluation of Moving Map Displays of Ownship on the Airport Surface DOT/FAA/AR-04/39. DOT-VNTSC-FAA-04-11. Cambridge, MA: US DOT Volpe Center. Available at www.volpe.dot.gov/hf/pubs.html.

www.ingramcontent.com/pod-product-compliance
Lightning Source LLC
Chambersburg PA
CBHW081845280526
45789CB00007B/2571